NEA
EARLY CHILDHOOD
EDUCATION SERIES

Moving Toward An Integrated Curriculum In Early Childhood Education

Dianne Lawler-Prince

Jennifer L. Altieri

Mary McCart Cramer

A NATIONAL EDUCATION ASSOCIATION
P U B L I C A T I O N

961552

Printing History
First Printing: July 1996

Note
The opinions expressed in this publication should not be construed as representing the policy or position of the National Education Association. Materials published by the NEA Professional Library are intended to be discussion documents for educators who are concerned with specialized interests of the profession.

This book is printed on acid-free paper.   This book is printed with soy ink.

ACID FREE
∞

Library of Congress Cataloging-in-Publication Data

Lawler-Prince, Dianne
        Moving toward an integrated curriculum in early childhood education / Dianne Lawler-Prince, Jennifer L. Altieri, Mary McCart Cramer.
        p. cm.—(NEA early childhood series)
        "A National Education Association publication."
        Includes bibliographical references.
        ISBN 0-8106-0367-5 (alk. paper)
2. Curriculum planning — United States.   3. Interdisciplinary
II. Cramer, Mary McCart III. Title.   IV. Series: Early childhood Education
Series
(Washington, D.C.)
LB1139.4.L39   1995
372.21—dc20   95-42453
                                                                        CIP

CONTENTS

PREFACE

A truly integrated curriculum is a goal every early childhood educator should strive for, but achieving this goal will take time, practice, and a team effort. We wrote this book to share knowledge and ideas about developmentally appropriate teaching practices.

Our collective professional experiences include researching, planning, and teaching integrated curricula. We also bring to this book years of responsibility for training preservice and in-service teachers to move toward integrated thematic teaching. We are pleased to share these experiences, along with perspectives from practicing classroom teachers and pre-service teachers.

Each chapter begins with an analogy that touches on both the topic of gardening and thematic teaching. These analogies are designed to help readers view moving toward curriculum integration as a "growth" process, one that takes place over time. This book compares the theme of gardening with the methods, strategies, and materials needed for learning about and "growing" your capacity to teach a more integrated curriculum.

We hope readers will take these ideas into the classroom, nurture them, and watch them flourish!

ACKNOWLEDGMENTS

The authors would like to thank the practicing classroom teachers and preservice teachers who contributed to the writing of this manuscript. Each group or individual is recognized, following the appearance of his or her materials or ideas, and they are listed in the section "Special Thanks to Contributors" at the end of this volume. We would also like to thank Timothy Crawford of the NEA Professional Library for his support, encouragement, and belief in this book.

THE AUTHORS

Dianne Lawler-Prince is associate professor of early childhood education at Arkansas State University, Jonesboro, Arkasas, and author of *Parent-Teacher Conferencing in Early Childhood Education,* published by the NEA Professional Library.

Jennifer L. Altieri is assistant professor of elementary education at Boise State University, Boise, Idaho.

Mary McCart Cramer is associate professor of elementary education at Arkansas State University, Jonesboro, Arkansas.

THE ADVISORY PANEL

Bill Blair, Kindergarten Teacher, Cascade Elementary School, Chehalis, Washington.

Doreen Jameson Burwell, First Grade Teacher, Pearl Sample Elementary School, Culpepper, Virginia.

Jean I. Caudle, Professor of Education, University of Wisconsin, Oshkosh, Wisconsin.

Lorna Hockett, Fifth Grade Teacher, Waldport Elementary School, Waldport, Oregon.

Chapter 1

INTRODUCTION:
PLANNING YOUR GARDEN PLOT

Gardens don't just happen. Gardens are planned—based upon previous experiences, research, observations, and preferences of the gardener. Like gardens, teaching doesn't just happen. Like gardeners, teachers must make many decisions. They select materials, choose instructional methods, and conduct classroom teaching based upon previous experiences, research, observations of other teachers, and the outcomes desired by the teacher, students, parents, and school administrators.

Teaching requires careful planning. Freiberg and Driscoll (1992) suggest that planning accomplishes many important goals. It makes learning purposeful, facilitates good management and instruction, provides for sequencing and pacing, links classroom events with community resources, provides for a variety of instructional activities, and establishes a repertoire of instructional strategies. Planning is also the key to making teaching more individually appropriate for children.

CLASSROOM PRACTICES PAST AND PRESENT

A book published by the National Association for the Education of Young Children (NAEYC), Bredekamp's (1987) *Developmentally Appropriate Practice in Early Childhood Programs Serving Children from Birth Through Age Eight,* produced a great deal of discussion, controversy, and questioning about how teachers and administrators could more appropriately teach children in "individually appropriate" and "age appropriate" ways.

In the past, schools were preoccupied with using "teacher-proof" materials, but now teachers face important decisions regarding not only the content to be taught but also the most effective strategies to teach the content. Bredekamp's landmark book inspired schools to address such curricular issues as:

(1) providing for all areas of a child's development—physical, emotional, social, and cognitive—through an integrated approach; (2) emphasizing learning as an interactive process, including active exploration and interactions with peers, materials, and adults; (3) emphasizing learning activities and materials that are real, concrete, and relevant; (4) including children's interests in the planning process; and (5) providing a variety of materials and activities. Although stated broadly, these guidelines were sanctioned by NAEYC, the largest and one of the most influential early childhood organizations in the United States.

Although the practices Bredekamp recommends were not embraced by all educators, it is hard to argue with the following list of *in*appropriate K-3 practices gleaned from his book.

1. Curriculum is narrowly focused on the intellectual domain, without recognition that all areas of children's development are interrelated.
2. All children are expected to read at grade level and their performance is measured by standardized tests.
3. The curriculum is divided into separate subjects, and primary emphasis is given to reading and secondary emphasis to math.
4. Instructional strategies primarily include teacher-directed reading groups, lecturing, whole-class discussion, and paper and pencil practice or worksheets.
5. Teachers use planning time to prepare and correct worksheets.
6. Children are expected to work silently and alone most of the time.
7. "The goal of the reading program is for each child to pass the standardized tests given throughout the year."
8. "Math is taught as a separate subject at a scheduled time each day."
9. Social studies, science, health, art, music, and physical education are taught infrequently and as separate subjects. (Bredekamp, 1987. pp. 70-72)

In essence, Bredekamp identified many traditional school practices as inappropriate. As a result, educators began to take a critical look at what was going on in traditional classrooms.

MOVING TOWARD CURRICULUM INTEGRATION

Bredekamp also outlined specific guidelines for *appropriate* K-3 practices. These guidelines provide teachers with important information to assist in making decisions about what should take place in classrooms.

1. "The curriculum is integrated so that children's learning in all traditional subject areas occurs primarily through projects and learning centers that teachers plan and that reflect children's interests and suggestions." (p. 67)
2. Learning occurs in meaningful contexts.
3. Skills are taught as needed.
4. Children work cooperatively in small groups or individually in learning centers and on projects.
5. Children select activities themselves or are guided by the teacher to make appropriate selections.
6. "Learning materials and activities are concrete, real, and relevant to children's lives."
7. Work places and spaces are provided for children to work and play. These places are used flexibly.
8. Language, literacy, math, science, social studies, health and safety, art, music, movement, woodworking, drama, and dance are integrated throughout the curriculum as well as throughout the day.
9. "Multicultural and nonsexist activities and materials are provided to enhance individual children's self-esteem and to enrich the lives of all children with respectful acceptance and appreciation of differences and similarities." (Bredekamp, 1987. pp. 67-72)

Bredekamp's book has been influential with change-minded teachers and administrators in schools across our nation. Routman (1991) says that the movement to more meaning-based and student-centered approaches is growing steadily. Teachers are being empowered to make important decisions not only about what young children will learn, but also how they will go about the learning process and how the learning will be evaluated.

Sometimes teachers have good ideas and good intentions, but they lack the confidence and time to integrate subjects, activities, materials, and content. But an abundance of materials has been published to assist teachers with the implementation of developmentally appropriate practices. Today, teachers are aware of such appropriate practices as learning centers, whole language, and cooperative learning. By reading, attending workshops, conferences, and classes, many have become inspired to incorporating these practices into their classroom routines. In addition, the teacher's manuals for basal reading series have begun to include materials and practices associated with the whole-language movement.

Another approach to implementing developmentally appropriate practices is *curriculum integration* through thematic teaching—a form of teaching that has been practiced for many years. Clark and Yinger (1979) found that teachers considered "thematic unit" designs the most important type of planning. More recently, Fredericks, Meinbach, and Rothlein (1993) and Krogh (1990) recommended integrating or "webbing" the curriculum around thematic topics or through children's literature.

"WEBBING" AND "THEMATIC UNITS" DEFINED

Although we, the authors of the book you are reading, give more details in Chapter 4, we want to state at the outset that the terms "webbing" and "thematic units" are not synonymous. Both are forms of thematic teaching, but in this book, the term "thematic unit" is used in the broadest sense—the theme or topic is developed first and then the activities are integrated around the theme. When we talk about "webbing," we mean those activities (including the process of planning, the graphic representation of the connections, and the actual teaching of the webbed activities) that are based around a single piece of literature. We like Bromley's (1991) definition of *webbing*:

> In nature, a web is a network of fine threads that a spider weaves. This network forms a complicated structure that is the means by which the spider snares its prey. A web can also be a complicated work of the mind that represents objects or concepts and the relationships a person perceives among them. In a classroom, the term *web* borrows something from both definitions. A semantic web, used as an instructional tool in a classroom, is a graphic representation or visual display of categories of information and their relationships. (p.2)

Both approaches, webbing and thematic units, are equally

valid, but how can they be used by teachers in school districts where reading series have already been purchased and teachers are required to use them? What about teachers who have been teaching just the basic skills and using only phonics to teach reading? What about inexperienced teachers who lack confidence and the planning skills necessary to master the astronomically complicated task of integrating the entire curriculum without guidelines or how-to books? We believe textbooks should not be thrown out until teachers are able to see carefully nurtured "gardens" starting to take root.

SUMMARY

Creativity and the development of ideas are key aspects of teaching. Many people choose teaching as a career, not for the pay they receive, but for the rewards (enjoyment) they receive in the very process of teaching.

Planning for teaching is one of the most important roles of the classroom teacher (Clark & Yinger, 1979). Unlike the plants used in gardening, human beings are much more valuable resources and much more fragile. Teachers, unlike gardeners, cannot "replant" children; they must take them where they are and help them develop into healthy learners. One major goal of teachers in today's classrooms is nurturing children to help them feel whole, capable, competent, and a part of, according to Routman (1991), a community of learners.

The primary goal of this book is to introduce teachers to practical and realistic ideas for integrating the curriculum. We wanted to create a tool that is not only appropriate for novice teachers, but also for experienced teachers who want to restructure their teaching methods. Many veteran teachers find themselves frustrated or unable to do so.

In the past, many teachers considered whole language a complete methodology. Our premise in this book is that the ideas, concepts, and strategies that are a part of whole language can be used in any classroom. This book is intended to empower and challenge teachers to move toward curriculum integration as an effective and exciting instructional strategy. Throughout the book, we recommend ways for making learning meaningful, real, and relevant for children, ways that are practical and realistic for the teachers planning and teaching them.

The next chapter examines reading-series stories and sug-

11

gestions for webbing or integration that appear in those reading series. When teachers begin to think and plan for integration, they may begin with the basal readers and expand their thinking and planning with time and experience. Unfortunately, teachers often become overly ambitious, or they are pressured into jumping wholeheartedly into thematic teaching before they are ready. They are not prepared for the time, energy, and effort required to implement such a complex teaching method in the classroom. Basal readers can provide a foundation or springboard that teachers can use to work toward curriculum integration. Chapter 2 encourages teachers to begin the integration process and offers helpful suggestions for getting started.

Chapter 3 helps teachers bridge the gap between using the basal reader and using a completely integrated thematic curriculum. The chapter provides examples of literature that correlate with the broadly based themes, which can be used as springboards for the suggested activities. You will also find some sample curriculum webs designed by primary-grade teachers.

Chapter 4 includes thematic units and webs designed by classroom teachers, positive examples of what can and should happen in primary-grade classrooms.

Chapter 5 addresses the selection and use of quality literature when creating curriculum webs. Also included are suggestions for using literature in nontraditional ways.

Chapter 6 reaffirms the fact that teachers have the knowledge, the power, and the ability to adapt the ideas presented in this book and make them work in their individual classrooms. The chapter ties together the ideas presented in this book to enable those who are working toward integrating the curriculum to feel empowered to make decisions that are appropriate to their situations.

The book concludes with an annotated bibliography.

Gardens are based on creativity and ideas developed over time. Viewing other gardens may inspire the garden planner to implement new or innovative ideas. Gardeners often visualize the garden, its appearance at various stages, and the outcomes or harvest of the season. Decisions made by the gardener are based on terrain, soil, temperature, sunlight, and so on. Careful planning goes into the design. Getting seeds or small plants off to a good start is one of the most important aspects of gardening. Many gardeners will admit that the reward or success of the garden is in the *process* of gardening itself.

REFERENCES

Bredekamp, S. *Developmentally Appropriate Practice in Early Childhood Programs Serving Children From Birth Through Age Eight.* Washington, DC: National Association for the Education of Young Children, 1987.

Bromley, K.D. *Webbing with Literature.* Boston: Allyn and Bacon, 1991.

Clark, C. and Yinger, R. "Teachers' thinking." In P.L. Peterson & H. L. Walberg (Eds.), *Research on Teaching.* Berkeley: McCutchan, 1979.

Fredericks, A.D., Meinbach, A.M., and Rothlein, L. *Thematic Units.* New York: Harper Collins, 1993.

Freiberg, H.J., and Driscoll, A. *Universal Teaching Strategies.* Boston: Allyn and Bacon, 1992.

Krogh, S. *The Integrated Early Childhood Curriculum.* New York: McGraw-Hill, 1990.

Routman, R. *Invitations: Changing as Teachers and Learners K-12.* Portsmouth: Heinemann, 1991.

Chapter 2

USING BASALS: PREPARING THE GROWING MEDIUM

"As much as sunlight and rain are among gardeners' strongest natural allies, weeds and pests can be their greatest natural foes." (Time-Life, 1991)

Planting the first garden, like planning an integrated curriculum for the first time, takes experience and knowledge. Just as beginning gardeners often start off with small plots and expand, so, too, do many teachers take small steps when attempting an integrated curriculum for the first time. Those first steps toward integrating a curriculum are almost always the hardest. By making a commitment to try to integrate the content areas, teachers are moving in the right (developmentally appropriate) direction.

THE CHANGES IN BASAL READERS

For many years, teachers have considered the basal to be an important part of elementary classrooms. Even today, many teachers can remember the name of the basal series that they used in elementary school and can name some of the stories in them. Although the idea of using a basal, defined as a textbook used to teach beginners, in the reading class is not new, the contents of the basal have changed tremendously over the years.

Originally, many basals underrepresented women and minorities (Deay & Ribovich, 1979; Spencer & Dee, 1978). Also, the portrayal of minorities and elderly people (Deay & Ribovich, 1979) was unrealistic. Critics faulted not only the illustrations, but also the text. Many people felt that the stories were uninteresting (Spencer & Dee, 1978) and that the language was stilted (Chall, 1983). It was common to see the vocabulary so controlled that the dialogue was unrealistic (Gourley, 1978). Many people can remember reading sentences like this: "Go Dot! Go Jim! Go Spot! Go! Go! Go!" The early basals had many inadequacies. Over the past decade, their content has changed dramatically.

Now, readers notice bright, attractive pictures that portray people in nonstereotypical roles. Also, publishers use quality stories written by popular children's authors. For example, the second-grade basal published by Harcourt Brace Jovanovich (HBJ), includes stories written by Patricia Reilly Giff, Nikki Giovanni, and even Joan Blos. Publishers are also including multicultural stories and a variety of genres: nonfiction, fantasy, poetry, and others.

The practice of "basalizing" literature, that is, modifying the original story to meet the text limits imposed by a reading series, seems to have diminished. In HBJ's second-grade basal, the publishers used many picture books as originally written. Aside from deleting some pictures, as was the case in *I Love Saturday* by Patricia Reilly Giff (1989), HBJ kept the text of many stories the same. When a story was not reprinted in its entirety, as in the case of "Junk Day on Juniper Street" by Lilian Moore (1991), the publishers alerted the reader. The new basals are a welcome change from the older versions.

Not only are the student editions of published reading programs different today, but the teacher's editions are also different. In the 1970s and 1980s, the teacher's manual often told the teacher exactly what to say and when to say it. Teachers were led to believe that the publisher knew best how to teach reading in the classrooms. The publishers also explicitly laid out the steps the teachers needed to follow in order to teach the reading lesson (Woodward, 1985). The amount of thinking required of the teachers was minimal.

Current texts are different. The newest editions of basals not only use published literature and a less-controlled vocabulary, but they also use a less authoritarian tone in the teacher directions (Hoffman et al., 1994). The publisher provides ideas and offers the teacher a number of activities to select from, depending upon the needs of the children. The teacher's editions commonly suggest ways to tie together reading with language, spelling, listening, speaking, and writing. No longer does the basal publisher expect the teachers to rely on separate spelling and language guides to teach the other concepts. Instead, the basal often cites language concepts and writing ideas that can be correlated with the individual stories. Story vocabulary is often recommended as a useful source of spelling words for the children. HBJ even includes additional reference materials containing ideas to involve the family and to help meet the needs of English as a Second Language (ESL) learners.

Accompanying materials for the teachers are not limited to worksheets, workbooks, and reference manuals; teachers often receive big books. While some of these big books are replications of stories in the basal, others are supporting material for the series. Sometimes the materials include supplementary books that the children or teachers can read to expand on the themes found in the stories. Finally, many series now include a writer's journal or notebook for teachers that encourages creative writing. The publishers also recommend that teachers include other types of journal writing in their classrooms.

Basals are still found in many classrooms and used by most elementary teachers (Walmsley & Walp, 1989) for a variety of reasons. First, many school districts still require teachers to use the basal to teach reading (Routman, 1991). Ideally, teachers should have a choice in the materials selected to teach reading, but many teachers who have the opportunity to choose still prefer the basal. Teachers who have taught for years, often enjoy the security of the basal. It is familiar material with which they are comfortable. For beginning teachers, the basal provides a variety of stories and ideas at their fingertips. While teaching is never easy, the use of a basal means that teachers have materials at hand and do not need to search for stories to use with their students (Reutzel, 1996).

THE BASAL AS A SPRINGBOARD

The positive aspects of the current basal reading series make the basal a logical starting point for developing an integrated curriculum. Rather than having the children simply read stories from the basal during a discrete segment of the day, you can use the basal as the springboard for a variety of learning experiences. Children should not come to view reading as a wholly separate activity in the school day, because this makes learning less relevant. Integration of content areas is a vital aspect of the developmentally appropriate practices necessary in today's schools (Bredekamp, 1987).

Experiences in life never occur in isolation. People often use strategies from mathematics, writing, reading, and other content areas to solve problems. A person reads newspaper advertisements and decides what to buy, in part, because of the price of the goods. That person uses knowledge about reading, writing, and mathematics to solve the problem of formulating a shopping list.

Traditionally, schooling has not provided children with practice in these kinds of meaningful tasks. Integrating all aspects of the curriculum provides for real, relevant, and enjoyable learning. Integration helps bring the real world into the classroom.

An integrated curriculum is not only developmentally appropriate, but also has been recommended for a variety of children including gifted students (Swartz, 1991), learning disabled students (Staab, 1991; Swicegood & Parsons, 1991), and ESL students (Irujo, 1990). Teachers can feel confident that an integrated curriculum will best meet the needs of their children regardless of their abilities. Integrating the curriculum has been shown to improve comprehension (Erwin, 1992), and, if used properly, can help children develop higher-level thinking skills. With an integrated curriculum, children can be allowed to make decisions about their learning and provided the means to enhance their self-esteem through cooperative learning. The benefits of an integrated curriculum are many and teachers can begin to reap rewards if they use their basals efficiently. This means using the basal as a springboard to develop an integrated curriculum.

INITIAL ATTEMPTS AT INTEGRATING THE CURRICULUM

Developing an integrated curriculum is never easy, yet many teachers are making initial attempts to do so. In fact, most teachers are taking the suggestions in the teacher's editions of the basals and integrating spelling, language, and reading. They are teaching language concepts with each story and using the vocabulary words as spelling words. Often, these teachers are calling this an integrated curriculum.

On the following pages we offer four fictitious vignettes that provide examples that are similar to what really happens in classrooms. In a way, these are examples of what not to do.

Teacher Vignette #1—Maria

Consider Maria. She is in her second year as a full-time teacher. Her school district adopted the HBJ reading series. She attended two summer in-service training sessions that were designed to assist her in the implementation of the reading program in this series. Maria began the school year with a great deal of uncertainty about how to address all the children's needs, how to schedule activities throughout the day, and how to cover material in a timely manner.

Maria's second-grade students are reading *Arthur's Pet Business*, by Marc Brown (1990), in the basal reading series. During language arts, Maria is focusing on the publisher's suggested language skill that accompanies the story. Today her students are writing a story about what would happen if they started their own business to earn money for something they wanted. In spelling, her children learn the words *allowed, care, earned, phone, special,* and *work*. Her spelling test is not composed of 10 words found on a grade-level word list but is made up of vocabulary words from the story.

Yet, Maria wonders what more she could be doing.

Assessment of Maria's Situation

Maria can feel proud of her attempts at combining the language arts. Change is never easy, but Maria is willing to get started in moving toward an integrated curriculum. The important thing to remember is that her effort is only a beginning step toward integration.

There are several disadvantages associated with this type of integration, however. First, Maria artificially segments the time for spelling, language, and reading during the class schedule. For example, even though the vocabulary words are taught as spelling words, there is still a separate time set aside for spelling. Also, although Maria is trying to integrate the language arts, she teaches other content areas, such as mathematics, science, social studies, and health, in traditional ways. Each subject is taught separately and not tied into the language arts. The basal often serves as a crutch for this type of planning.

Maria is also unsure of her role as decision maker. Instead of using the knowledge she and her children possess, she merely uses the suggestions provided by the basal publisher.

Although there are weaknesses associated with this type of teaching, there are strengths that can be further developed. Since Maria tried to show students that spelling, reading, and language are related, this method of teaching is making learning more meaningful. For example, students no longer study a spelling list of unfamiliar words each week. Instead they learn words that they encounter in context. Also, Maria has made a promising start by spending time planning how to effectively use the basal.

A MORE INTEGRATED CURRICULUM

A slightly more integrated model would require that the teacher make an attempt to tie in more than the language arts areas. The teacher might incorporate some aspect of science, math, health, and social studies along with the basal.

Teacher Vignette #2—Martha

Let's look at Martha. Martha has 16 years of public school teaching experience. She has taught fourth, fifth, and sixth grades prior to moving to the first-grade level. She works closely with the other three first-grade teachers on thematic unit planning.

Martha plans to incorporate science into the new reading series. Her students have just read "Vegetables," from *Lionel at Large* by Stephen Krensky (1986), in their basal reader. Martha decides to integrate science by discussing gardening. The children discuss each type of food mentioned in the story. Martha lists each food on the board, and her students brainstorm to add their favorite foods to the list. Her students mark which foods could be grown in the soil. Next the children research how each type of food is planted and harvested. Martha is planning a special surprise by having a local gardener come to speak to the class, as a culminating activity for the unit.

Teacher Vignette #3—Ed

Ed has five years of second-grade teaching experience. His educational background includes a bachelor's degree in science. He received a master's degree in science education in elementary education three years ago. Ed feels strongly that science concepts must be included as important facets of the curriculum. However, Ed feels very unprepared to teach using the new series.

Ed's second-grade students have just finished reading *Little Penguin's Tale* written and illustrated by Audrey Wood (1989). That has always been Ed's favorite story, so he likes to tie it in with other subject areas. Today he is using the story to discuss zoo animals in science.

After his students finish reading the story, Ed has them look at the penguin picture in the basal. The students brainstorm to come up with other types of animals they might see at a zoo, and Ed lists each type on a chart board. Ed, who has already thought out the lesson, is able to provide interesting information on several types of zoo animals and show books that contain pictures of the animals in their habitats. He discusses physical characteristics of various animals (e.g., webbed feet, fur, feathers). After the list is made, each child chooses a favorite animal and draws its picture. They write a few sentences about the animal they chose. These pages are assembled to make a personalized zoo book for the class library.

Assessment of Martha's and Ed's Attempts at Integration

Although both Martha and Ed are attempting thematic teaching using their new reading series, there are major weaknesses in their attempts. To begin with, the skill selected is often an obscure aspect of the actual story. In Martha's case, gardening is a remote link to the foods discussed in the story "Vegetables." The book only discusses the foods, yet she makes the leap to gardening because she has a predetermined topic she wants to cover. There is no meaningful relationship between the topic covered and the basal story. Although, her planning can be conceptualized as moving from the general to the more specific, the linkage is not strong enough.

Ed, likewise, does not choose a theme that adequately correlates with the story *Little Penguin's Tale*. Although a penguin is mentioned in the story, the story is not designed to teach about the broad topic of zoo animals. Ed's use of science as a starting point is fine, but he should have a more narrow focus. Once again this type of planning is conceptualized as thematic, but the focus of the story is too narrow.

Both of the stories can be used to teach and integrate other content areas, but the integration needs to be carefully planned by the teacher. "Vegetables" would be better used in teaching about food groups and nutrition. *Little Penguin's Tale* would be an excellent resource to use in teaching about polar animals and animals living in cold climates. The important thing to remember is that *the concept should be evident in the story* and not merely a tenuous link based on the need to find a relationship between the story and the concept.

Martha and Ed should be commended, however, for their honest attempts to correlate content areas with the reading program. By thoughtfully considering the concepts to be taught and the stories used, these teachers can move on to more adequately integrated curricula. Of course, one concern of teachers attempting to integrate the content areas with the reading series is the need for assistance and planning. It is much easier to teach each subject in isolation than to analyze different subjects and draw meaningful links between them. Just as teaching becomes easier with time and practice so does the skill of integrating the curriculum.

THEMATIC UNITS AS SPRINGBOARDS FOR USING BASALS

The third type of integration commonly found in classrooms, is a slightly more complex model than those previously described. This type of integration is practiced by teachers who use a thematic unit as the springboard for planning and incorporating the basal.

Teacher Vignette #4—Terrance

Terrance, with his 12 years of teaching experience, feels competent in thematic teaching. Terrance often works for the school district during the summer conducting in-service training for incoming teachers. He served on the basal adoption committee and was a strong advocate for using the basal in the district. Terrance is a second-grade teacher and the primary-grade team chair for his school district.

Each year, Terrance teaches a unit on "Neighbors." Due to his meticulous organization, he can quickly and efficiently locate the files in his cabinet that contain the activities for the unit. This spring is no different. After retrieving the social studies files related to neighbors, Terrance sits down and selects the story "Junk Day on Juniper Street" by Lilian Moore (1991) and the poem "Neighbors" by Mary Ann Hoberman (1993), both of which are found in his basal. These texts clearly deal with the concept of neighbors. He then uses the basal to tie in language, spelling, and reading. Terrance is ready to start teaching.

Assessment of Terrance's Planning Techniques

Unlike Maria, Martha, or Ed, Terrance is clearly further along toward his goal of integrating the curriculum. Not only does he choose stories because of the contribution that they can make to the teaching of the theme or topic, but Terrance also includes a variety of content areas. Basically Terrance has good ideas, and with greater understanding of the integration process, he will be able to achieve his goal.

Like many teachers though, he is integrating through the

subject area of social studies. Teachers like Terrance often integrate through social studies or science themes and keep mathematics isolated. In fact, mathematics seems to be the most difficult subject for teachers to integrate into the curriculum. Yet, it must be included for integration to be complete.

Another major weakness in Terrance's plan for teaching is that he has used the thematic unit before. While repetition in itself is not wrong, merely reproducing an entire unit each year is not the best way to teach. No two classes are the same. Teachers must modify their plans on a yearly basis. Optimal learning can occur only when teachers take into consideration the children in the class, societal changes, and developmentally appropriate practice.

Another important aspect of developmentally appropriate practice is the direct involvement of the children. Children should participate in the planning process for the unit. They need to feel that they are a vital part of the classroom. Involvement starts with the planning of the unit and the concepts to be taught. Their interests, backgrounds, and the region in which they live are all important considerations of thematic planning.

Generally, new basal series include stories that are adaptable and practical for use in this type of teaching. Problems arise, however, in the conceptualization of the theme. Teachers must use the stories included in the basals but also plan to weave them into the broad topic (theme). A great deal of planning, along with some reflective thinking, must occur for this method to be implemented successfully.

CONCLUSION

Many teachers can identify with one of the teachers described in the vignettes in this chapter. They can recognize their own weaknesses and see some ways they can turn them into strengths. Each scenario has positive aspects and areas that can be strengthened. This book aims to show that basals can be used as springboards for an integrated curriculum. By using familiar materials, teachers can become much more secure in experimenting with integrated curricula. The important thing to remember is: Never give up.

This text identifies some excellent children's books and the annotated list at the end of this book provides numerous resources to help teachers develop integrated units. Teachers can begin this process by recognizing and celebrating the degree to which they currently integrate their curricula and by making a commitment to develop a more fully integrated curriculum.

REFERENCES

Bredekamp, S. *Developmentally Appropriate Practice in Early Childhood Programs Serving Children From Birth Through Age Eight.* Washington, DC: National Association for the Education of Young Children, 1987.

Brown, M. *Arthur's Pet Business.* New York: Little, Brown & Co., 1990.

Chall, J. *Learning to Read: The Great Debate.* New York: McGraw-Hill, 1983.

Deay, A.M. and Ribovich, J.K. "Portrayal of the Elderly in Basal Readers. *Reading Psychology,* 1(1), 32-40, 1979.

Erwin, B. *The Effect of Culturally Related Schemata and Instruction Using Thematic Units on Comprehension.* (Eric Document Reproduction Service No. ED 349 540), 1992.

Fredericks, A.D., Meinbach, A.M., and Rothlein, L. *Thematic Units,* New York: HarperCollins, 1993.

Giff, P.R. *I Love Saturday.* New York: Puffin Books. 1991.

Gourley, J. W. "This Basal is Easy To Read or Is It? *Reading Teacher,* 32(2), 174-182, 1978.

Hoberman, M.A.. "Neighbors" in *Poems of Friendship: I Like You, You Like Me* by M.C. Livingston. New York: MacMillan, 1993.

Hoffman, J.V., McCarthey, S.J., Abbott, J., Christian, C., Corman, L., Curry, C., Dressman, M., Elliott, B., Matherne, D., Stahle, D. "So What's New in the New Basals? A Focus on First Grade." *Journal of Reading Behavior,* 26(1), 1994.

Irujo, S. *How To Plan Content-based Teaching Units for ESL.* (ERIC Document Reproduction Service No. ED 320 452), 1990.
Krensky, S. "Vegetables," from *Lionel at Large.* New York: Dial

Books for Young Readers, 1986.

Krogh, S. *The Integrated Early Childhood Curriculum*. New York: McGraw-Hill, 1990.

Moore L. *Junk Day on Juniper Street and Other Easy to Read Stories*. New York: Parents' Magazine Press, 1991.

Reutzel, D.R. and Looter, R.B. *Teaching Children to Read: From Basals to Books* (2nd ed.) Englewood Cliffs, N.J.: Merrill, 1996.

Routman, R. *Invitations: Changing as Teachers and Learners K-12*. Portsmouth, NH: Heinemann., 1991.

Spencer, H. & Dee, A. "Smile and the World Smiles with You: A Comment on Basal Readers. *Phi Delta Kappan*, 60(3), 252-253, 1978.

Staab, C. Classroom Organization: Thematic Centers Revisited. *Language Arts*, 68(2), 108-113, 1991.

Swartz, E. (Ed.). Thematic Instruction. *Communicator*, 21(4), 1991.

Swicegood, P.R., & Parsons, J.L. "The Thematic Unit Approach: Content and Process Instruction for Secondary Learning Disabled Students." *Learning Disabilities Research and Practice*, 6 (2), 112-116, 1991.

Time-Life. *Complete Guide to Gardening and Landscaping*. New York: Simon & Schuster, 1991.

Walmsley, S.A. & Walp, T.P. *Teaching Literature in the Elementary School: A Report of a Project on the Elementary School Antecedents of Secondary School Literature Instruction* (Report No. CS212-135). (ERIC Document Reproduction Service No. ED 315 754, 1989.

Wood, A. *Little Penguin's Tale*. San Diego: Harcourt Brace & Co, 1989.

Woodward, A. *Taking Teaching out of Teaching and Reading out of Learning To Read: A Historical Study of Reading Textbook*

Teachers' Guides, 1920-1980. Paper presented at annual meeting of the American Educational Research Association, 1985.

Chapter 3

USING TEXTBOOKS MORE EFFECTIVELY: TOOLS FOR YOUR GARDEN

A gardener may use a tiller, a hoe, a spade, a rake, a wheelbarrow, a waterhose, as well as many other tools. Each has a specific use but might also serve other purposes. To be effective and efficient, the gardener and the teacher must make the best use of their tools. These tools can be used in creative or innovative ways.

TEACHING IN THE PRIMARY GRADES

Educators in schools that are moving toward curriculum integration must consider time, as well as opportunity, for long-range planning of the curriculum. When discussing the ideas we explore in this book with teachers, the authors discovered that, although integrating the curriculum is something that many teachers want to do, the actual implementation can be troublesome. First-grade teachers report experiencing difficulty in selecting activities from each unit and activities to go along with each story.

Sometimes, teachers must begin with advocacy. That is, they must advocate for planning time and grade-level team meetings. Teachers can make a case for the importance of this time spent in planning, particularly if they are willing to share the outcomes (thematic units) with other teachers and parents.

Children in first grade need opportunities for hands-on learning. They learn through their senses, through concrete experiences, and by active participation with manipulatives. When teaching reading, teachers must make the materials meaningful and find ways for students to make connections between real-life situations and learning.

First-grade teachers must place a greater emphasis on developmental characteristics and meeting individual needs so that children's initial attempts at reading and other subject-area learning are successful. Children today usually attend preschool and kindergarten, yet as first graders they continue to bring varied experiences into the classroom. Home and family experiences are an important part of the curriculum. Teachers can enhance the curriculum by putting a greater emphasis on these experiences.

Expectations of second graders are far greater than in years past. Standardized tests continue to drive the curriculum and push the academic content down from upper grades into second grade. Teachers, children, and parents experience stress from the pressure of the fast-paced curriculum in second grade.

In third grade the emphasis shifts to reading and comprehending content area material. These skills are deemed important because third graders need to gain independence, seek new information, and extend their reading and listening vocabulary. Third graders encounter a number of concepts in the content areas that are not a part of their oral vocabularies. Thus, learning often becomes more difficult for children who experience difficulty in reading (i.e., those who are reading below grade level).

Unfortunately, administrators, teachers, and parents tend to overlook the developmental needs of third graders. According to Piaget's (1959) theory, the majority of primary grade children are still in the concrete operational stage. Abstract thinking and problem-solving activities present problems for these children. Therefore, they need meaningful, concrete activities and materials that actively involve them in the learning process so that their learning attempts are successful (Bredekamp, 1987).

BASAL: USING WHAT WE HAVE

When using a basal series, teachers must carefully select the activities for integrating the curriculum. Although the teacher's editions may recommend math, science, social studies, art, as well as other content area activities, many of these recommendations "stretch" the story theme. They may also be inappropriate for children within a specific region or include vague and ambiguous ideas.

Teachers who are teaching in school districts that have adopted "new" basal reading series are expected to use these tools to the best of their ability. This means that teachers must draw from their previous experiences. In addition, they examine the materials and make selections from what is available to them.

If basals are what you have available, go ahead, use them. But you can also transform your lessons into meaningful integrated thematic activities by creating webs.

WHY WEBS?

This book recommends webbing as the way to bridge the gap between using only basal-based planning and creating a fully integrated thematic curriculum. Webbing is a powerful tool. Teachers just beginning to do integrated thematic teaching can create a web to easily integrate, for example, music, math, art, and social studies with a story from the basal reader. The graphic representation of the web also provides an eye-pleasing "outline" of the thematic activities.

As teachers move toward more fully integrated thematic units, the webs evolve. At the center of a basal-based web (duration of, let's say, one day) is the title of the story from the basal reader. The center of a full-blown thematic unit (duration: one week or more, sometimes much more) is the theme itself. A thematic unit can also be graphically depicted in a web format (see Figure 5.1, on page 83 for an impressive example).

BRIDGING THE GAP USING BASALS AND WEBS

The HBJ third grade, Level 2 reading text, *A Most Unusual Sight* (Farr & Strickland, 1994), includes the story "Owl Moon" by Jane Yolen. This story could be used in curriculum webbing. The teacher's edition recommended activities (see Figure 3.1) that correlate additional subject areas with the reading, spelling, and language activities. Altieri and Lawler-Prince recommend these additional activities that could be integrated along with this story.

- *Social studies*—students could interview adult males (fathers). They could write interview questions concerning winter sports, favorite types of hunting, and winter hobbies. Children could proofread and work with partners to refine their interview questions.

- *Math/Graphing*—students could use the interview results and design a graph of various hobbies, sports, and types of hunting.

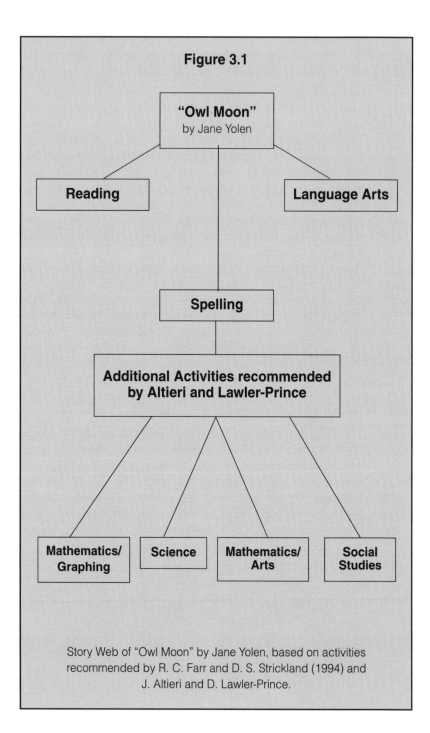

Figure 3.1

"Owl Moon"
by Jane Yolen

Reading

Language Arts

Spelling

Additional Activities recommended
by Altieri and Lawler-Prince

Mathematics/
Graphing

Science

Mathematics/
Arts

Social
Studies

Story Web of "Owl Moon" by Jane Yolen, based on activities
recommended by R. C. Farr and D. S. Strickland (1994) and
J. Altieri and D. Lawler-Prince.

- *Science*—teacher could provide information (research) about various types of owls. Working in groups, children could compare and contrast the distinguishing characteristics of a selected owl with those of the Great Horned Owl. The students could complete a Venn diagram comparing and contrasting these two types of owls.

- *Math/Art*—teacher could research types of animal tracks and provide information about the size and shape of tracks. Working in groups, students could use the information to create tracks and design maps with directions for following the tracks.

These activities integrate the curriculum around the theme of the selected story, "Owl Moon." One reason teachers use basal stories as a springboard is that the material is readily available to them. Building upon previous teaching experiences they make decisions about themes and activities based upon the selected story. There are limitations to this method, however. Teachers must engage in a great deal of planning, research, and gathering of materials prior to the introduction of the story. As you will see from the examples below, using a single story as the focus of the web also limits the amount of quality activities that can be developed around its theme.

EXAMPLES OF TEACHER-CREATED WEBS

The following examples depict teachers' webs that have been implemented in primary classrooms.

First Grade: A "My Friends Web"

Lisa Metz, a first-grade teacher at Hillcrest Elementary in Jonesboro, Arkansas, designed a web (Figure 3.2) with activities that correlate with the theme of the story "My Friends" by Taro Gomi. This story is included in the HBJ grades 1-2 reading book, *A Friend Like You* (Farr & Strickland, 1993). The HBJ series recommends additional children's literature as "companion books" to *A Friend Like You*. *Coco Can't Wait* by Taro Gomi (1985) (easy), *The Mixed-up Chameleon* by Eric Carle (1975) (average), and *Elmer* by David McKee (1989) (challenging) are three stories that

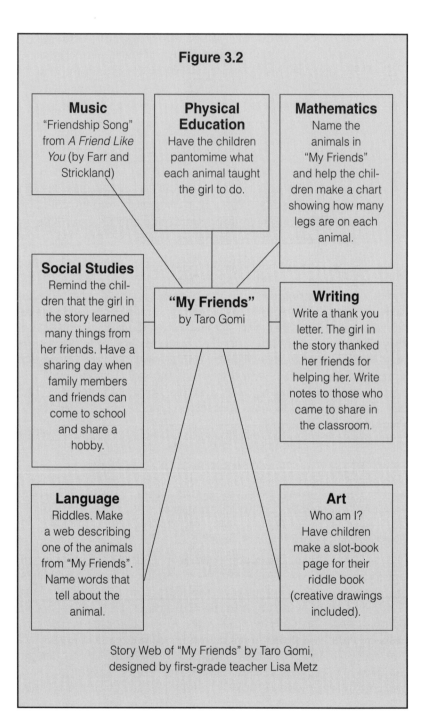

Figure 3.2

Music
"Friendship Song" from *A Friend Like You* (by Farr and Strickland)

Physical Education
Have the children pantomime what each animal taught the girl to do.

Mathematics
Name the animals in "My Friends" and help the children make a chart showing how many legs are on each animal.

Social Studies
Remind the children that the girl in the story learned many things from her friends. Have a sharing day when family members and friends can come to school and share a hobby.

"My Friends"
by Taro Gomi

Writing
Write a thank you letter. The girl in the story thanked her friends for helping her. Write notes to those who came to share in the classroom.

Language
Riddles. Make a web describing one of the animals from "My Friends". Name words that tell about the animal.

Art
Who am I? Have children make a slot-book page for their riddle book (creative drawings included).

Story Web of "My Friends" by Taro Gomi, designed by first-grade teacher Lisa Metz are also recommended because of their emphasis on positive self-image. "My Friends" is introduced in a chapter entitled "Just Like Me." Additional stories, poems, and songs that are a part of this unit are: *Quick as a Cricket,* Audrey Wood (1990) (fantasy); *Honey, I Love,* Eloise Greenfield (1986) (poem); *I Eat My Gumdrops,* Freya Littledale (1993) (poem); and *Willoughby, Wallaby, Woo,* Dennis Lee (1993) (song).

As you can see in Figure 3.2, Ms. Metz chose to include a song, a movement activity, a categorizing (mathematics) activity, writing, riddles, art, and guest speakers. Through these activities that correspond with the content areas, first graders can learn even more about the concepts emphasized in this story. They can learn about friendship, learning, and hobbies from the activities developed in other content areas that supplement the reading material. Ms. Metz used the "Big Book" when reading the story with the children.

Second Grade: A "Mitchell is Moving" Web

In another unit, second-grade teachers, Jane Mills, Joyce Neff, Cheryl Reeves, Kimberly Rouse, and Kay Sloan at North Elementary School in Jonesboro, Arkansas, used the story "Mitchell is Moving," by Marjorie Weinman Sharmat, illustrated by Jose Aruego and Arianne Dewey, from the HBJ second-grade text, *Up One Hill and Down Another* (Farr and Strickland, 1993). The teachers emphasized the concepts of letter writing, moving, and the postal service. (See Figure 3.3.)

To develop geography/social studies skills, children were asked to identify distances on a map, and "pretend" they were moving to different regions. This activity also incorporated mathematics because they examined mileage and distances between cities. Furthermore, children wrote a letter to themselves as a class. They addressed it "Dear Us" and everyone signed it. Children were introduced to letter writing formats in this activity.

As a continuation of the letter-writing activity, children visited the post office. The Jonesboro city post office was within walking distance of their school. They saw the basket in which mail was dumped and the sorting machine that arranged the mail according to zip code. They learned about the importance of letter sealing and stamping mail.

Following this field trip, children wrote thank you letters to the post office staff. Teachers developed a word bank of possi-

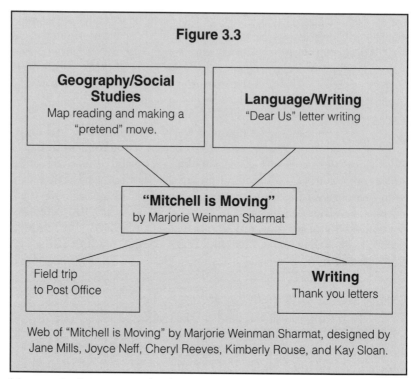

Figure 3.3

Geography/Social Studies
Map reading and making a "pretend" move.

Language/Writing
"Dear Us" letter writing

"Mitchell is Moving"
by Marjorie Weinman Sharmat

Field trip
to Post Office

Writing
Thank you letters

Web of "Mitchell is Moving" by Marjorie Weinman Sharmat, designed by Jane Mills, Joyce Neff, Cheryl Reeves, Kimberly Rouse, and Kay Sloan.

ble words for use in the letters and displayed the bank on the board. Children mailed the letters to the postal workers.

Teachers reported one problem with this story—a line stating that the main character moved "two weeks away." This phrase was abstract and the children were unable to relate to a specific town or distance that the character moved.

These teachers liked the suggested material in the teacher's edition and establishing a routine of activities around each story, each week. (They present one story per week and include as many of the recommended activities as possible during that time frame.)

They also liked taking the spelling words from the text of the reading materials. These teachers believe that the words, when taken from the context of the story, are more meaningful. They may also be more difficult to spell than words with particular vowel and consonant patterns. They liked exposing children to the words in more than one place—spelling and reading. They believe that having high expectations of the children promotes higher achievement.

In addition, the school's Title I reading teachers coordinate their work with the children by introducing story vocabulary words one week prior to the introduction of a particular story. In this approach, children with reading difficulties will have been introduced to the words prior to reading the story. The teachers find this to be an effective method of working with children who have difficulties in reading.

When asked how they are able to coordinate their activities, second-grade teachers at North School said that they plan in teams during their break times—lunch, recess, music, P.E., and so on. They have obviously made personal and professional commitments to work as a team in this effort to integrate the curriculum.

The second graders made shirts (see Figure 3.4a) following the introduction of *I Love Saturday* by Patricia Reilly Giff, illustrated by Frank Remkiewicz. The children drew pictures of things that they love.

Ms. Mills' children also drew murals of what they thought Greenwich Village would look like. Figure 3.4b depicts these Arkansas children's "image" of Greenwich Village.

Kittie Mickle, an Arkansas State University student, conducted a lesson on contractions to coordinate with *I Love Saturday*, because there are 15 different contractions in the story. Her lesson introduced children to "Potsy," the apostrophe. The children enjoyed learning about "Potsy" and the lesson increased their awareness of contractions.

Ms. Rouse introduced the concept of *alliteration* through the use of the character's name, Jessica Jean.

Third Grade: A "Johnny Appleseed" Web

Mona Broadway, a third-grade teacher at South Elementary in Jonesboro, Arkansas, designed a web (Figure 3.5) that incorporated activities around the theme of "Johnny Appleseed" following the reading of "Johnny Appleseed," retold and illustrated by Steven Kellogg, in *Like a Thousand Diamonds* (Farr & Strickland, 1993). This story is a part of a unit entitled "Being Special" and is presented in the text under the theme (heading) "Improving the World." Other stories in this theme are: *Miss Rumphius* by Barbara Cooney and *A Seed Is a Promise* by Claire Merrill. Books recommended for additional reading about making improvements include: *The Chalk Box Kid* by Clyde Robert Bulla (1987) and *Frederick* by Leo Lionni (1987).

Ms. Broadway included the idea of a "character tree,"

Figure 3.4a. T-shirt design.

which involved the construction of a cardboard tree in her classroom. Students were asked to write a characteristic about John Chapman (Johnny Appleseed) on a paper apple and hang it on the character tree. Students then used the characteristics to write a paragraph about John Chapman.

The story was introduced in the fall, so apples were readily available. Other activities that correlated nicely with this story were: (1) science activities of examining the growth of the apple and the parts of a plant, cooking with apples, and studying the food

Figure 3.4b. Murals inspired by "I Love Saturday."

36

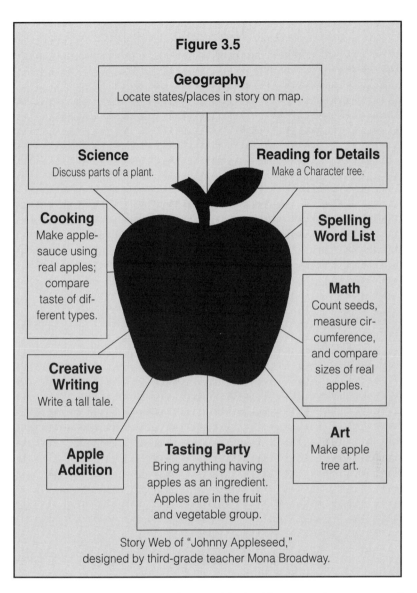

Figure 3.5

Geography
Locate states/places in story on map.

Science
Discuss parts of a plant.

Reading for Details
Make a Character tree.

Cooking
Make apple-
sauce using
real apples;
compare
taste of dif-
ferent types.

**Spelling
Word List**

Math
Count seeds,
measure cir-
cumference,
and compare
sizes of real
apples.

**Creative
Writing**
Write a tall tale.

**Apple
Addition**

Tasting Party
Bring anything having
apples as an ingredient.
Apples are in the fruit
and vegetable group.

Art
Make apple
tree art.

Story Web of "Johnny Appleseed,"
designed by third-grade teacher Mona Broadway.

groups (particularly "Fruits and Vegetables"); (2) geography activities of locating and other map skills; and (3) writing activities of creating a tall tale. Art was emphasized and the spelling word list was drawn from words in the story.

EXPANDING ON WHAT BASALS OFFER

When teachers attempt to integrate the curriculum using any of the new basal reading series, they face the age-old, but very real, problems of scheduling, materials, planning time, and lack of support. They express concerns about their ability to effectively implement the suggested activities in a timely manner. Teachers also report a lack of training in using this method of teaching.

Themes Not Included in the Basal

There are many exciting and relevant themes that are not included in a basal reading series. Even when they are just beginning to web using the basals, teachers can develop their own themes by using regional resources, additional textbook materials, and stories, poems, and songs from children's literature. For example, in Dubuque, Iowa, several third-grade teachers planned and implemented a thematic unit entitled "Treasures of the Mississippi." Dubuque is located on the Mississippi River and the teachers used this natural resource as the basis for their web.

Iyla Ant, Brenda Janco, Mary Kane, Christine McCarron, and Eleanor Ray of Table Mound Elementary School in the Dubuque Community School District Expeditionary Learning Project planned and implemented the activities (Figure 3.6) that correlate with the Houghton Mifflin social studies text *From Sea to Shining Sea,* Chapter 1 (1991). Their use of the river as a teaching tool was innovative and regional by design. They integrated the concepts of boating and swimming safety as a part of this study. The culminating activity of "floating your boat on the river" was carried out as a field trip with songs and cooking (wiener roast, etc.). Other practical life activities such as doing a river-bank clean-up project or developing a public service announcement on the importance of taking care of the river could be incorporated into this hands-on learning activity. A follow-up to this field trip included reviewing, writing, and problem solving.

You should note that through Expeditionary Learning (a grant funded by Outward Bound), the Dubuque third-grade teachers cited above were given four and one-half days of release time to plan this thematic unit. Substitute teachers covered their classes while they planned the unit. Additional funding for resource materials and field trips was available through their grant. These teachers designed and conducted a professional pre-

Figure 3.6

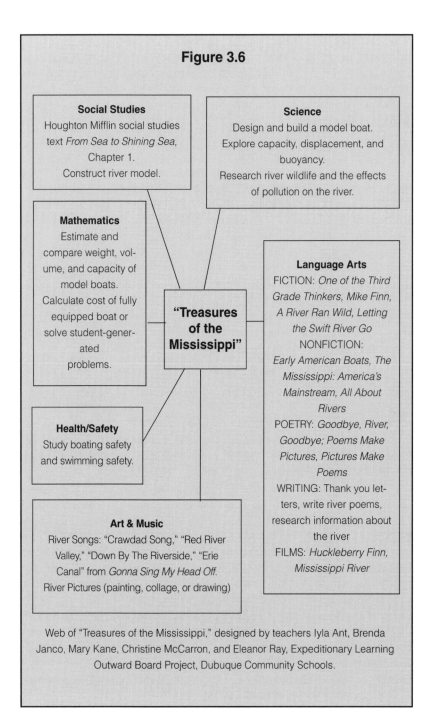

Social Studies
Houghton Mifflin social studies text *From Sea to Shining Sea,* Chapter 1.
Construct river model.

Science
Design and build a model boat. Explore capacity, displacement, and buoyancy.
Research river wildlife and the effects of pollution on the river.

Mathematics
Estimate and compare weight, volume, and capacity of model boats. Calculate cost of fully equipped boat or solve student-generated problems.

"Treasures of the Mississippi"

Language Arts
FICTION: *One of the Third Grade Thinkers, Mike Finn, A River Ran Wild, Letting the Swift River Go*
NONFICTION: *Early American Boats, The Mississippi: America's Mainstream, All About Rivers*
POETRY: *Goodbye, River, Goodbye; Poems Make Pictures, Pictures Make Poems*
WRITING: Thank you letters, write river poems, research information about the river
FILMS: *Huckleberry Finn, Mississippi River*

Health/Safety
Study boating safety and swimming safety.

Art & Music
River Songs: "Crawdad Song," "Red River Valley," "Down By The Riverside," "Erie Canal" from *Gonna Sing My Head Off.*
River Pictures (painting, collage, or drawing)

Web of "Treasures of the Mississippi," designed by teachers Iyla Ant, Brenda Janco, Mary Kane, Christine McCarron, and Eleanor Ray, Expeditionary Learning Outward Board Project, Dubuque Community Schools.

sentation for the news media, parents, school board members, administrators, and other classroom teachers. The presentation included a skit as well as visual aids to explain their conceptualization of "Treasures of the Mississippi." Thus, these teachers were accountable to the whole community for the time spent planning this unit.

Other Concerns About Basals

Classroom teachers with whom we have worked have expressed some concerns about integrated thematic teaching with basals. One concern is that many of the stories listed under a theme (in a basal reader) are not related closely enough to the theme to effectively integrate the subject areas and activities. Using only the preselected literature is limiting, because stories included in the basal are not always age-appropriate or regionally appropriate. When provided with these teaching materials, teachers sometimes feel an obligation to use them in sequence and exclusively. Furthermore, if you want children's input in curriculum planning, you will have difficulty including children in the planning process when the basal dictates every move.

BEGINNING TO CREATE THEMATIC UNITS

A Web Based on the Theme "Transportation"

Using multiple stories, poems, anthologies, and so on, connected to a theme or topic is a more powerful option along the continuum of curricular integration. For example, *All Through the Town,* published by Silver, Burdett, and Ginn (1994), includes stories, poems, and songs for first grade, around the theme of "Transportation." The authors designed a web (Figure 3.7) by selecting a variety of stories that could be used to teach about transportation. The theme of "Transportation" was selected because of its popularity as a topic in kindergarten and primary grades. Additional children's literature that correlates with the theme includes: Kovalski's *Wheels on the Bus* (1974), *Truck* by Donald Crews (1980), *Zip, Whiz, Zoom!* by Stephanie Calmenson (1992), or Roger Yepsen's *City Trains* (1993). Poetry collections for children on transportation include *Sing a Song of Subways,* by Eve Merriam (1983); *Song of the Train,* by David McCord (1974); Sylvia Cassedy's *Zoomrimes* (1993), and Myra Cohen Livingstone's *Roll Along: Poems on Wheels* (1993)

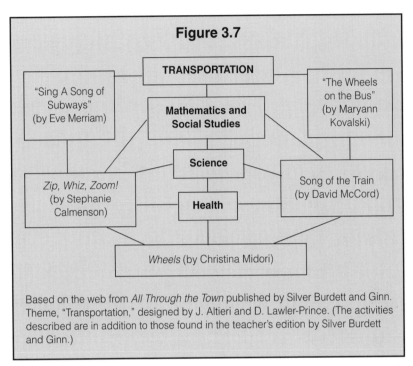

Figure 3.7

TRANSPORTATION

"Sing A Song of Subways" (by Eve Merriam)

Mathematics and Social Studies

"The Wheels on the Bus" (by Maryann Kovalski)

Science

Zip, Whiz, Zoom! (by Stephanie Calmenson)

Health

Song of the Train (by David McCord)

Wheels (by Christina Midori)

Based on the web from *All Through the Town* published by Silver Burdett and Ginn. Theme, "Transportation," designed by J. Altieri and D. Lawler-Prince. (The activities described are in addition to those found in the teacher's edition by Silver Burdett and Ginn.)

Other activities in math, social studies, science, and health that correlate with the theme are:

- *Math and social studies*—Students can graph the types of transportation they use to get to school (walking, car, truck, bus, subway, train, etc.). Teacher can discuss the concepts of *more, less,* and *equal.*

- *Science*—Students can examine pictures (photographs) of types of emergency and/or public transportation. Students should pay close attention to the color of the vehicle. Have each child draw a picture of one emergency and/or public transportation vehicle. Children can write about why the vehicle is painted the designated color (for safety), for example, red fire trucks, white police cars.

- *Health*—Class can discuss healthy ways children use transportation. They can explore ways in which children can use transportation without adult assistance

41

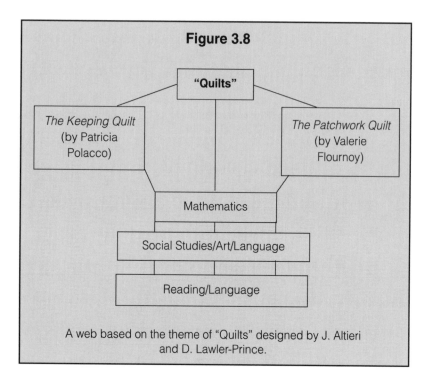

Figure 3.8

"Quilts"

The Keeping Quilt (by Patricia Polacco)

The Patchwork Quilt (by Valerie Flournoy)

Mathematics

Social Studies/Art/Language

Reading/Language

A web based on the theme of "Quilts" designed by J. Altieri and D. Lawler-Prince.

and discuss activities that are healthy and safe—walking, bicycling, skating, and so on.

A Web Based on the Theme "Quilts"

Teachers have the right as well as the responsibility to select children's literature that pertains to a theme. *The Keeping Quilt (1988),* written and illustrated by Patricia Polacco, included in HBJ's (1993) third-grade reader, *A Most Unusual Sight,* is one example. Third-grade teachers may use this story along with *The Quilt Story* by Tony Johnston and Tomie dePaola (1992), and *The Patchwork Quilt* by Valerie Flournoy (1985). These stories could be clustered together under the theme of "Quilts" or "Traditions." The authors have designed activities (see Figure 3.8) that integrate the curriculum around this theme.

- *Mathematics*—working in cooperative groups, children use wallpaper sample books and select four to six patterns of wallpaper and tear them from the book. They then cut the wallpaper using the line markings on the back of the wallpaper (older children using rulers may be able to design rectangles, triangles, diamonds, and other shapes using the wallpaper). After cutting the wallpaper shapes, each group designs a pattern on a I4 x I4-inch paper square. Each group's quilt block can be added to form a whole group quilt.

- *Social Studies/Art/Language*—the teacher invites parents and grandparents to bring in family heirloom quilts and discuss patterning, applique, embroidery, and piecing. Then the teacher has students draw designs of quilts and attempt to describe their designs. These drawings and descriptions can be put together in a class book. Children examine the class-made book and vote on a design for a class quilt. (This is truly an integrated activity because content from various subject areas is included.)

- *Reading/Language*—after the children examine the quilts brought into the classroom, they brainstorm descriptive words to form a "word bank." Students can design their own pattern and describe the pattern in words so that a partner can recreate the pattern. Partners look at drawings and descriptions to make comparisons.

MAKING APPROPRIATE DECISIONS WHEN MOVING TOWARD INTEGRATION

Arkansas State University graduates in early childhood education and elementary education are surveyed to determine their expertise. Recent graduates have expressed satisfaction and a certain comfort level with webbing. Also teachers who have completed in-service training and who are advocates of the whole language approach seem to be better prepared for this type of teaching than those who lack training in whole language methods.

Some teachers with several years of teaching experience who have primarily used a phonetic approach or a basic phonics approach have expressed concerns about omitting specific skills instruction. Some have reverted to the old methods with which they were comfortable, including spelling lists of words with commonalities (make, take, bake, cake, shake, rake). These same teachers are frustrated by the lack of curriculum integration training and preparation time.

Confidence in one's decision-making abilities is a necessary aspect of teaching today. In the past, textbook writers designed materials that required little or no decision making on the part of the teacher. Many of the new reading series include suggested/required activities and several optional ones. Because the curriculum has been so test-driven, teachers continue to feel the pressure for their children to perform, so activities designated as optional in the text are considered mandatory by the teachers. The transition into a new way of teaching is a slow process because teachers must change thinking patterns.

SUMMARY: STEPS TO GET STARTED WITH WEBBING

There are several steps necessary to get started in webbing successfully.

1. Choose a story in the reading text that you really like. Base your selection on your prediction of how children will respond to the story. Think about the available resources in your region.
2. Read the optional activities offered by the textbook authors.
3. Plan additional activities that closely correlate with the story's theme.
4. Draw a web and ask yourself the following questions:
   a. Do these activities closely relate to the theme of the story?
   b. Would these activities be individually and age appropriate for the children in my classroom?
   c. Do I have the available resources to effectively carry out my plans?
   d. Does my daily/weekly schedule allow time for these activities?
   e. Are there any other text materials that could be correlated with this story (e.g., Houghton Mifflin mathematics)?

REFERENCES

Bredekamp, S. *Developmentally Appropriate Practices for Children Ages Birth Through Age Eight.* Washington, D.C.: National Association for the Education of Young Children, 1987.

Bulla, C.R. *The Chalk Box Kid.* New York: Random House, 1987.

Calmenson, S. *Zip, Whiz, Zoom!* Boston: Jay Street Books, 1992.

Carle, E. *The Mixed-up Chameleon.* New York: Harper Collins Children's Books, 1975.

Carse, R. *Early American Boats.* New York: World Publishing Co., 1968.

Cassedy, S. *Zoomrimes: Poems About Things That Go.* New York: Harper Collins, 1993.

Cherry, L. *A River Ran Wild.* New York: Harcourt Brace Jovanovich, 1992.

Cooney, B. *Miss Rumphius.* New York: Viking Children's Books, 1982.

Crews, D. *Truck.* New York: Greenwillow, 1980.

Emil, J. *All About Rivers.* Mahwah, NJ: Troll, 1984.

Farr, R.C., and Strickland, D.S. *A Friend Like You.* New York: Harcourt Brace Jovanovich, 1993a.

————. *Like a Thousand Diamonds.* New York: Harcourt Brace Jovanovich, 1993b.

————. *Up One Hill and Down Another,* New York: Harcourt Brace Jovanovich, 1993c

————. *A Most Unusual Sight.* New York: Harcourt Brace Jovanovich, 1994.

Flournoy, V. *The Patchwork Quilt.* New York: Dial Books for Young Readers, 1985.

Giff, P.R. *I Love Saturday.* New York: Puffin Books, 1991.

Gomi, T. *Coco Can't Wait.* New York: Puffin Books, 1985.

Greenfield, E. *Honey, I Love and Other Love Poems.* New York: Harper Collins Children's Books, 1986.

Huckleberry Finn. 16mm, 45min. Morris Plains, NJ: Lucerne, 1980.

Hougton Mifflin. *From Sea to Shining Sea.* Boston: Houghton Mifflin, 1991.

Johnston, T. and dePaola, T. *The Quilt Story.* New York: Putnam Publishing Group, 1992.

Kellogg, S. "Johnny Appleseed." In R.C. Farr and D.S. Strickland (Eds.), *Like a Thousand Diamonds.* New York: Harcourt Brace Jovanovich, 1993.

Kovalski, M. "The Wheels on the Bus." Boston: Little, Brown & Co., 1974.

Kuell, K. *Gonna Sing My Head Off.* New York: Alfred Knopf, 1992.

Lee, D. "Willoughby, Wallaby, Woo." In Farr, R.C. and D.S. Strickland, *A Friend Like You.* Orlando: Harcourt Brace Jovanovich, 1993.

Lionni, L. *Frederick.* New York: Knopf Books for Young Readers, 1987.
Littledale, F. "I Eat My Gumdrops" In Farr, R.C. and D.S. Strickland *A Friend Like You.* Orlando: Harcourt Brace Jovanovich, 1993.

Livingstone, M. *Roll Along: Poems on Wheels.* New York: Macmillan Children's Group, 1993.

McCord, D. "Song of the Train." In *One at a Time: His Collected Poems for the Young.* Boston: Little, Brown & Co., 1974.

McKee, D. *Elmer.* New York: Lothrop, Lee & Shepherd, 1989

Mendoza, G. *Goodbye River, Goodbye.* Garden City: Doubleday, 1971.

Merriam, E. "Sing a Song of Subways." In Jack Prelutsky, Ed. *Random House Book of Poetry for Children.* New York: Random House, 1983.

Mississippi River. 16mm, 16 min. Morris Plains, NJ: Lucerne, 1980.

Piaget, J. *Language and Thought of the Child.* (M. Gabrain, trans.). New York: Humanities Press, 1959.

Polacco, P. *The Keeping Quilt.* New York: Simon & Schuster, 1988.

Rimanelli, G. *Poems Make Pictures, Pictures Make Poems.* New York: Pantheon Books, 1972.

Silver, Burdett, and Ginn. *All Through the Town.* Morristown, NJ: Silver, Burdett, and Ginn, 1994.

Wood, A. *Quick as a Cricket.* Auburn, ME: Child's Play International, (1990).

Yepsen, R. *City Trains.* New York: Macmillan, 1993.

Yolen, J. *Letting the Swift River Go.* New York: Little, Brown & Co. 1992.

York, C. B. *Mike Fink.* Mahwah, NJ: Troll, 1980.

Chapter 4

CREATING THEMATIC UNITS: WARM SUN AND GENTLE RAIN

Just as these ingredients for a successful garden—sun and rain—are important, the ingredients for thematic teaching are of primary importance. Although a gardner doesn't have control over the amount of rain that falls during a season, he or she does determine the location of the garden plot, and in that selection, how much sun the plants will receive and whether the garden can be irrigated. Teachers determine necessary ingredients for thematic teaching and nurture those topics to help them grow and develop into quality thematic units with the materials and activities to accompany them.

FROM DEPENDENCE ON BASALS TO INTEGRATION

All teachers supplement the basal, but as they move away from the basal and toward integration, teachers develop broad topics and meaningful themes and select more relevant literature. Many even use the terms *webbing* and *thematic units* synonymously. For the purposes of this book, however, the terms are not used synonymously. The authors have referred to webbing as those activities based around a single piece of literature. Webbing also refers to using a basal or the text of another content area (science or social studies) as the springboard for activities that correlate with the theme, topic, or concept of the literature. Another example of webbing is the use of a single piece of children's literature with concepts and activities woven around the theme of that single book.

Dianne Lawler–Prince designed a web (Figure 4.1) to integrate the curriculum around *Sitting in My Box* by Dee Lillegard 1993. She describes activities in several subject areas and provides ideas for projects.

While a web is usually designed to be implemented in a

Figure 4.1

Reading
Provide large pasteboard boxes with pillows inside for reading "boxes." Cut the top flaps off the boxes (for lighting) and cut an opening for a door.

Math
Children measure different types of boxes (cereal, lunch boxes, shoe boxes, music boxes, etc.) and discuss length and width. Children might also enjoy using a tape measure to measure the "Reading Boxes."

Science
Class discusses and reads about fleas. A veterinarian might come to talk about treatment of animals for fleas.

Writing
Children write a story about reading their favorite book in a box. Ask them "What might join you in the box?"

Let the class write a "group story" about a giant box (provide one if possible) that several "real people" could get inside. Design the story around fantasy and reality. Have children draw a picture and write about what they would do if given a big box.

Science and Math
Students discuss and measure the size of the animals in the story. Measure their lengths and heights with yardsticks and tape measures. Plot them or diagram them on the parking lot—let the children walk around them as they would in a real zoo.

Sitting in My Box
by Dee Lillegard

Art
Children design a decorative box for a gift.

Let the children bring different types of boxes from home to create a display of boxes.

Use boxes for a diorama.

Social Studies
Discuss mailing packages to other cities and/or countries. A worker from UPS might come in to demonstrate what the company does in package delivery and service.

Projects
In cooperative groups, children design something using their box. Make a village from small boxes to go in the block building (Lego)™ center.

Web of *Sitting in My Box* by Dee Lillegard, designed by Dianne Lawler-Prince.

single day, or a few days, thematic units are planned for a week or longer. In this book, the term thematic unit is used in the broadest sense—the theme or topic is developed and the activities are integrated around the theme. Historically, thematic teaching has been encouraged. Child-centered education was first espoused by Rousseau. Pestalozzi also recommended that children needed "object lessons" rather than direct instruction. The ideas of many noted educators have influenced the movement toward thematic teaching. Krogh (1990) states "The teacher in a child-centered classroom must behave and think in ways different from a teacher whose primary purpose is to transmit knowledge" (p. 55). Children today, more than ever, need challenges and a stimulating environment in order to attract, maintain, and foster their attention and interests.

THEMATIC TEACHING

Thematic teaching of some type is one of the first requirements for a child-centered classroom. In the absence of thematic teaching, children must "shift gears" from subject to subject and use processing skills during and between each shift. This shifting is often counterproductive. Learning is much more powerful when students discover the intricate relationships between subjects and concepts and integrate that knowledge into a complex whole through thematic teaching (Krogh, 1990).

Campbell (1994) says:

> We have set a difficult mission for ourselves as we seek to teach in ways very different from the ways we may have been taught ourselves. We seek to organize our schools in ways that will promote and support students having many powerful learning experiences within their school day. We want our time with our students to matter now and for the rest of their lives...But once we remember how we learned best, we owe our students nothing less. (p.2)

For centuries, kindergarten and preschool teachers have taught through thematic units. They plan the themes, select children's literature to go with the theme, plan learning centers, field trips, and activities that are integrated with the central theme being taught. Young children who are taught using this method are able to make mental connections and make "sense" of what they are learning. Because this type of teaching is so powerful, teachers are beginning to attempt it in primary grades as well.

Unfortunately, there are misconceptions about thematic teaching. One is that the entire day must be restructured to facilitate thematic teaching. Flexibility and a schedule conducive to thematic teaching are ideal, but teachers should to try thematic teaching whatever their current teaching environment.

Another misconception is that a connection to a theme can be made with almost any piece of literature. This is unfortunate because many teachers attempt to make connections or to "integrate" using a piece of literature that is inappropriate (see Teacher Vignettes 2, 3, and 4 in Chapter 2). Teachers also misconstrue the terms *integration* and *correlation*. Although correlating activities with a piece of literature can be a beginning point for teachers, the goal is to integrate the curriculum around the theme or topic.

Differences Between Correlation and Integration

According to Routman (1991), integration means:

> that major concepts and larger understandings are being developed in social contexts and that related activities are in harmony with and important to the major concepts (p. 276).

Many times teachers purchase resource materials that include thematic ideas and activities already developed. They attempt to put these ideas and activities into place in their classrooms. The problem with these materials is that "there is often little, if any, development of important ideas. This is correlation, not integration" (Routman, 1991, p. 277). Concepts are superficial and forced or there is no important concept development. Another difficulty with these materials is that they may not be appropriate for the children in classroom. Topics and themes developed by teachers are likely to be most age-appropriate and individually relevant.

According to Routman (1991), in the integrated curriculum, "relationships among the subject areas or disciplines are meaningful and natural" (p. 277). In creating thematic units, the primary concerns are:

- developing attitudes
- oral language
- perspectives to be covered

- opportunities for social interactions
- the interrelationship of important concepts.

This list leads us to one of the most important aspects of thematic teaching—planning. Although we mentioned the importance of planning in Chapter 1 of this book, what follows is a more in-depth look at planning for effective integrated thematic teaching.

PLANNING FOR EFFECTIVE INTEGRATION

Planning is essential for effective integration. As Baker (1983) says:

Never take a trip without a map! You must plan every phase of the garden from layout to placement...Keep this plan after you've planted so you'll be sure to know where everything is; otherwise you may pull up the lettuce and cultivate the dandelions by mistake (p. 172–73).

When teachers begin to plan thematic units they often feel overwhelmed and burdened by such a daunting task. Time is a major factor. Teachers who plan in teams or groups often report finding the most effective tools, resources, materials, and ideas for teaching by brainstorming with their colleagues. Resources and references are helpful, but many important factors must be considered when attempting thematic teaching. Some resources are incomplete and not specific to a particular classroom, community, or region.

Freiberg and Driscoll (1992) suggest that designing entails putting mental plans into a blueprint for instruction. They recommend taking into account throughout the planning and teaching processes:
- the context of the teaching,
- the content to be taught,
- the learners involved, and
- the teacher (experiences, strengths, weaknesses, preferences, etc.).

Lawler–Prince (1993) developed a theory on teachers' conceptualizations of planning. This theory is based on observations of in-service and preservice teachers' lesson and unit plans,

53

previous teaching experiences, and review of the literature on planning techniques. In Type I planning (see Figure 4.2), teachers select a theme or topic, choose specific literature that would best teach the selected concepts and objectives of the theme, and then begin to plan the activities that are appropriate to integrate the activities with both the theme and the literature selected. Many kindergarten teachers, without the restraints of state-mandated guidelines or standardized testing, have used this type of planning for years.

In Type II planning (see Figure 4.3), the teacher begins with a set of objectives to address during a specified time frame, develops a theme or topic in which the objectives can be properly addressed, and then plans activities that match the theme and provide the "integration" of subjects or content areas around the theme. The final phase in this type of thematic planning is the literature selection. Although no planning method is "correct" or "incorrect," in Type II planning, the selection and use of literature plays a less significant role in the planning and teaching of the theme.

In Type III planning (see Figure 4.4), teachers select the

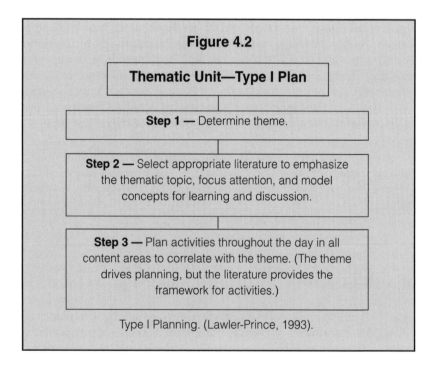

Figure 4.2

Thematic Unit—Type I Plan

Step 1 — Determine theme.

Step 2 — Select appropriate literature to emphasize the thematic topic, focus attention, and model concepts for learning and discussion.

Step 3 — Plan activities throughout the day in all content areas to correlate with the theme. (The theme drives planning, but the literature provides the framework for activities.)

Type I Planning. (Lawler-Prince, 1993).

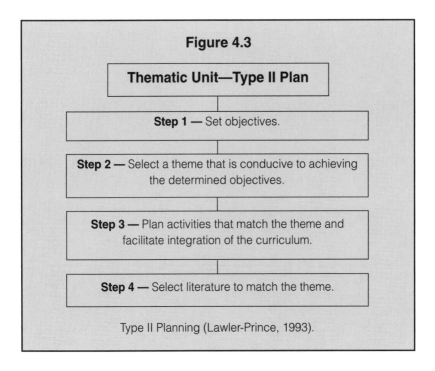

Figure 4.3

Thematic Unit—Type II Plan

Step 1 — Set objectives.

Step 2 — Select a theme that is conducive to achieving the determined objectives.

Step 3 — Plan activities that match the theme and facilitate integration of the curriculum.

Step 4 — Select literature to match the theme.

Type II Planning (Lawler-Prince, 1993).

literature and then develop a theme that is appropriate for the literature selection(s). (These authors contend that the two processes probably occur simultaneously—theme and literature selection go hand in hand.) Teachers then determine objectives, taking into consideration all of the aforementioned factors. The next step is planning activities that grow out of the literature and expand the concepts in the theme. While this type of planning could be used to develop long-term thematic units, please note that the usual outcome of this type of planning are mini–units and curriculum webs that may take place during a single day. The web designed around *Sitting in My Box* by Dee Lillegard is an example of this type of planning (see Figure 4.1).

The authors view Type I planning as requiring high-level thinking skills. Teachers begin to show a very high level of planning, thinking, and organizing when they: (1) begin by developing a theme; (2) make literature selections based upon the themes; and (3) plan to use literature to correlate with the theme and plan activities to integrate the curriculum around the theme.

Teachers often gather a bunch of books around a theme and plan activities around that topic. These activities may be fun,

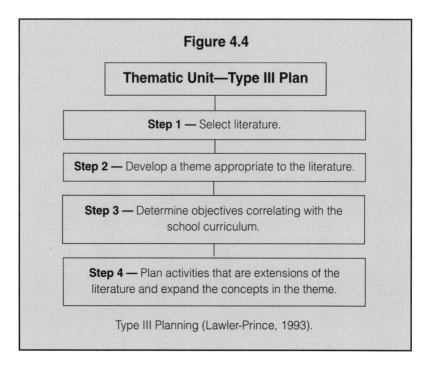

Figure 4.4

Thematic Unit—Type III Plan

Step 1 — Select literature.

Step 2 — Develop a theme appropriate to the literature.

Step 3 — Determine objectives correlating with the school curriculum.

Step 4 — Plan activities that are extensions of the literature and expand the concepts in the theme.

Type III Planning (Lawler-Prince, 1993).

but they will lack substance if they are not based on the major concepts in the theme. *Brown Bear, Brown Bear, What Do You See?* by Bill Martin, Jr., (1983) is an example of a poor selection for teaching the topic "Bears" to young children. The book, although a quality piece of children's literature, teaches nothing about the habitats, eating habits, or regions in which bears live. The book might be an appropriate selection for teaching children to identify colors.

Thematic teaching is, according to Routman (1991), "planning and teaching centered around a theme, topic, concept, or literature selection which is meaningful, real, and relevant to the children." (p. 276) A thematic unit may include, but is not required to include, all subject areas within the curriculum. It may also include extension areas, challenging activities, field trips for enrichment, and learning centers. Routman (1991) also says that:

a thematic unit is an integrated unit only when the topic or theme is meaningful, relevant to the curriculum, and students' lives, consistent with whole language principles, and authentic in the interrelationship of the language processes. (p. 278)

The thematic unit may only last for two to three days (a "mini-unit"); or one to two weeks (in traditional thematic format); or it may last up to six weeks (a "module"), particularly for older children. The breadth of the topic selected should determine the length of the unit. Broad topics such as "Environment," "Space," or "Plants" can be umbrellas for subtopic study. Thematic units based on these broad topics may last for several weeks.

EXAMPLES OF THEMATIC TEACHING

One example of a thematic unit was developed around the theme of "cooperation." The authors chose the unit "Gardening" (Lawler-Prince, et al., 1993) for its popularity, its appropriateness for various regions, and its relationship to the theme. The Gardening unit plan (see Figure 4.5) was developed for second- and/or third-grade students. First, the literature was selected around the theme. Then, activities were developed in each content area that would not only teach specific objectives of the unit theme, but would also expand the knowledge presented to the children through the literature selections. The content areas of social studies, mathematics, music, science, art, language arts, and movement were chosen for their appropriateness and relevance to this theme. The underlying purpose of the unit is to assist children in cooperating with one another and to teach them that teamwork is an important part of any group effort.

Christi Zielinski, a preservice teacher attending Arkansas State University, designed a curriculum web using Type III planning (see Figure 4.6) that is based on Mick Inkpen's *The Blue Balloon* (1990). She determined that *The Blue Balloon* teaches the concepts of "color," "size," "story sequence," "air," and "shape." She used this single piece of literature to plan a mini-unit and to develop materials and activities relevant to the theme of the book as well as the concepts it addresses. The unit could be further developed by teachers who want to use it as a starting point, by selecting any one of the concepts, choosing additional pieces of literature, planning the activities, and implementing them in a meaningful, relevant sequence. This mini-unit could become a full–blown thematic unit developed around one of the themes addressed in this piece of literature.

Although quality literature is often a central part of each thematic unit, it is not necessary to building a thematic unit. Not

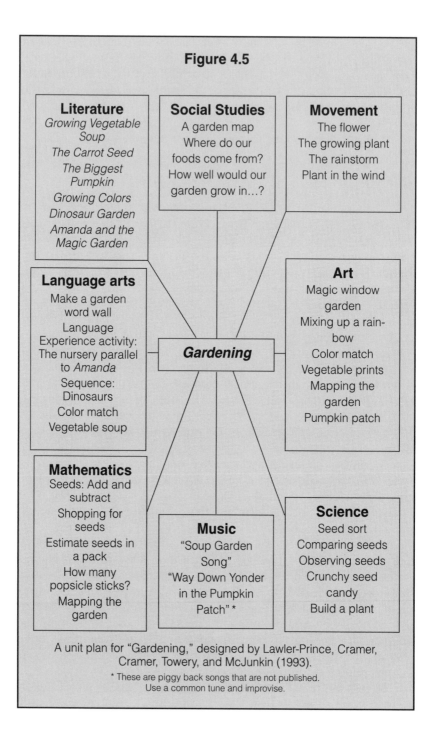

Figure 4.5

Literature
Growing Vegetable Soup
The Carrot Seed
The Biggest Pumpkin
Growing Colors
Dinosaur Garden
Amanda and the Magic Garden

Social Studies
A garden map
Where do our foods come from?
How well would our garden grow in…?

Movement
The flower
The growing plant
The rainstorm
Plant in the wind

Language arts
Make a garden word wall
Language Experience activity: The nursery parallel to *Amanda*
Sequence: Dinosaurs
Color match
Vegetable soup

Gardening

Art
Magic window garden
Mixing up a rainbow
Color match
Vegetable prints
Mapping the garden
Pumpkin patch

Mathematics
Seeds: Add and subtract
Shopping for seeds
Estimate seeds in a pack
How many popsicle sticks?
Mapping the garden

Music
"Soup Garden Song"
"Way Down Yonder in the Pumpkin Patch" *

Science
Seed sort
Comparing seeds
Observing seeds
Crunchy seed candy
Build a plant

A unit plan for "Gardening," designed by Lawler-Prince, Cramer, Cramer, Towery, and McJunkin (1993).

* These are piggy back songs that are not published. Use a common tune and improvise.

Figure 4.6

Story Sequence

Language arts—Make props to represent the scenes in the story. Let the children place the props in front of them as they retell the story.

Chart. Make a chart of other things the children think the balloon might do. Have the children draw a picture representing their ideas. Encourage them to write about their drawings.

Individual flannel boards. Make felt pieces for all the events in the story. First, have the children recall the events in the story and let them try to place the events in order on the felt boards.

Sequence puzzles. Glue drawings of the various events of the story on posterboard and laminate them. Have the children sequence the puzzle pieces.

Size

Mathematics—Have children order sets of balloons and other items in the book from smallest to largest.

Movement—Have children throw and catch various sizes of balloons to music. Have them follow their movements and let go and deflate their balloon, following its movement during deflation. (This should be done outdoors.)

The Blue Balloon
by
Mick
Inkpen

Air

Science—Have children blow soap bubbles, experimenting with blowing various size bubbles using different tools.

Color

Cooking—Have a blue party! Have the children help make blue gelatin following a rebus recipe chart. Set the table with blue plates, napkins, cups, and a centerpiece made of balloons.

Math—Have children finish color patterns of felt using colors as the sequencing format. (ex., blue balloon, yellow balloon, red balloon, ?? balloon (answer: blue balloon)

Science—Have children sequence paint chips from darkest to lightest.

Shape

Movement—Bean bag toss. Make the backboard in the shape of a big round balloon. Make the bean bags the various shapes of the blue balloon in the story.

Shape collage—Paste various shaped balloons on posterboard. Make similar ones for the children to velcro onto the board. The children can also design their own shape collages on construction paper.

Web of *The Blue Balloon* by Mick Inkpen (1990), designed by University of Arkansas preservice teacher Christi Zielinski.

every unit has to have literature. Cousins (1993) offers one such example from teacher Jane Klahsen. When one of Jane's first–grade children brought in a toad on the first day of school, she began to apply the Expeditionary Learning Principle of "The Having of Wonderful Ideas." (See Cousins, 1993) Jane encouraged her children to generate questions about what they would like to know about toads, to investigate these questions, and to answer them. Jane discovered that the children could not only answer their own questions about the toad, but also the questions raised by other students. At the end of the day, the class wrote and illustrated a book about toads. Jane says the activity is one of the most valuable "teachable moments" she has ever experienced.

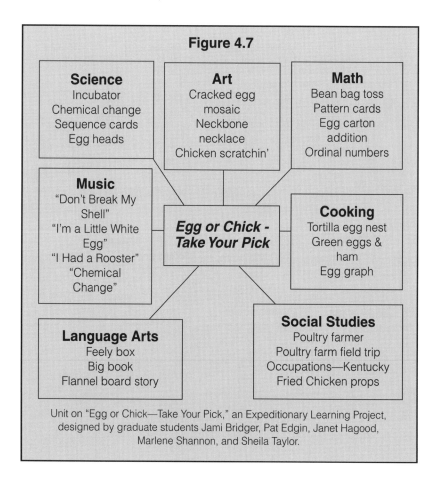

Figure 4.7

Science
Incubator
Chemical change
Sequence cards
Egg heads

Art
Cracked egg
mosaic
Neckbone
necklace
Chicken scratchin'

Math
Bean bag toss
Pattern cards
Egg carton
addition
Ordinal numbers

Music
"Don't Break My Shell"
"I'm a Little White Egg"
"I Had a Rooster"
"Chemical Change"

***Egg or Chick -
Take Your Pick***

Cooking
Tortilla egg nest
Green eggs & ham
Egg graph

Language Arts
Feely box
Big book
Flannel board story

Social Studies
Poultry farmer
Poultry farm field trip
Occupations—Kentucky Fried Chicken props

Unit on "Egg or Chick—Take Your Pick," an Expeditionary Learning Project, designed by graduate students Jami Bridger, Pat Edgin, Janet Hagood, Marlene Shannon, and Sheila Taylor.

Another group of teachers, participating in a graduate course, designed a thematic unit entitled, "Egg or Chick—Take Your Pick." This unit was fashioned after the types of units planned in Expeditionary Learning (see Chapter 3). Jami Bridger, Pat Edgin, Janet Hagood, Marlene Shannon, and Sheila Taylor planned activities and a field trip around the theme of "chickens and eggs" (see Figure 4.7). Although appropriate for kindergarten children, the theme, activities, and concepts could be adapted for first and/or second graders. These graduate students even wrote a song entitled "Don't Break My Shell" to the tune of Billy Ray Cyrus's "Achy Breaky Heart." Their group work was commendable as well as creative! They reported having a great deal of fun in the planning process as well.

Krogh (1990) provides some excellent examples and describes the planning process in developing these thematic units. She depicts a web or radial, which includes the content areas that may be included in each unit.

Particularly with older children (third graders), meaningful units can be developed around books by one author. A unit might also be developed around books with similar characters, or versions of folk/fairy tales. Krogh (1990) suggests a "storybook curriculum" in which teachers choose fairy tales and design the curriculum around the themes of each story. In the unit described here, the theme is "fairy tales," but the concepts taught could vary with the theme of the fairy tale taught that day. For example, with *The Little Red Hen,* "cooperation" might be the concept. On another day, *The Three Billy Goats Gruff* might emphasize anger, fear, and problem solving.

Through brainstorming and sharing ideas, teachers can begin to move toward an integrated curriculum. Through the examination of resources and relevant topics, teachers can also begin to bring the world into the classroom and more effectively take the classroom into the world.

INCORPORATING REGIONAL RESOURCES

Bredekamp (1992) says that "meaningful, real, relevant" topics and activities may be determined by the age level of the children being taught, the region in which they live, the background experiences of the children, and the relevance of the topic to the children's lives. For example, in Arkansas, farming is the primary occupation, yet many children have not been

61

exposed to or had the opportunity to study various types of farming within the state. In northeast Arkansas, cotton is a major crop. The children could visit the cotton fields in the fall, visit a cotton gin, and see a textile mill in which the cotton is woven into various materials. In northwest Arkansas, however, no cotton is grown. Chicken and cattle farming are the primary agricultural activities for that region. Children and teachers would have easy access to these resources when planning and teaching.

Teachers should look for books published locally to help them research local resources. The Southern Early Childhood Association's book *Exploring the Gulf Coast with Young Children: Authentic Activities and Projects for K–3 Classrooms* (Shores, 1993) provides teachers in the gulf coast region with ideas and resources. This is a wonderful way for teachers to begin exploring their resources, determining relevant and real topics for study, and planning for taking the classroom out into the community or region or bringing resources into the classroom from the community or region.

Brainstorming

When planning for thematic teaching, teachers should brainstorm, develop ideas, and conceptualize the relationships between the theme or topic and the relevance of the topic to the children's lives and examine materials and activities that can facilitate learning and make it a fun, exciting, worthwhile experience. Without brainstorming and careful planning, teachers often choose topics that are fragmented or lack meaning for the children. Some teachers feel that the topics suggested by the text books are the only themes that should be addressed in the classroom. When this happens, they miss the rewards that in-depth planning for thematic units can provide.

Three examples of *expeditions* (more elaborate thematic units that include visits or field trips to important sites related to the topic or theme) designed by classroom teachers are:

1. "Healthy Food Choices," a three-week unit designed by second-grade teachers Jean Corbett, Margaret Dettman, Lorie Duclas, Wendy O'Hara, and Nan Welch of Lincoln School in Dubuque, Iowa
2. "Light a Candle for Learning," a three–week unit for first graders, designed by Dorothy Lamb, Lisa Moldenhauer, and Sheila Lehman of Lincoln School in

Dubuque, Iowa, in which children explore the ways people mark and celebrate the passage of time in their lives. The unit's major project is hosting a birthday party for nursing home residents.

3. "Packed with Memories," a three-week unit designed for second graders by Bev Graves, Becky Campbell, and Nicole Lyon of Dubuque Community Schools, Dubuque, Iowa, which explores personal heritage, ancestry, and genealogy. The major project is making a quilt (Cousins, 1993).

Student Input

Especially during the development of regional-resources based units, students should have input, and their research, group participation, and interests may make these units some of the most valuable ones taught throughout the year.

Children (as well as the teacher) need to understand *why* the topic or theme is being studied, as well as the proposed outcomes of the study. The unit might even begin with a brainstorming session in which students identify questions regarding the topic and where the answers might be obtained. At the conclusion of the unit, the teacher needs to re-examine those questions and determine if the unit answered them all. If many interesting questions are unanswered, the teacher should consider further study. Flexibility is a key to planning, implementing, and following up thematic units.

Lawler-Prince (1994) created a thematic unit for which students could have a great deal of input (see Figures 4.8 and 4.9) entitled "My School as a Community." This unit, especially designed for third graders, could involve the students in learning about their school, as well as recognizing that their school is a community within itself.

Kimbro, Freeman, and Tennison (1994) developed an in-depth, award-winning unit called "There's No Place Like Home" (see Figure 4.10 for a partial list of subtopics, activities, and ideas in this unit). These first- and second-grade teachers of University Heights Elementary School in Jonesboro, Arkansas, won third place in the Primary Division of the 1994 International Paper Company Foundation's National Awards for Teaching Economics. The unit is primarily a study of people and animals—their shelters and homelessness. Their existing curriculum included the study of animal types, their habitats, families, and communities. The teachers decided to add economics. The children were involved in the design, production, and marketing of a product (refrigerator magnets) to be sold to raise money for their community service project—a donation to the homeless fund. The study lasted throughout the school year and incorporated all content areas. It is an example of a well-planned, integrated thematic unit. The sample activities and objectives provided here represent only a portion of the unit and its contents.

"Our first- and second-grade children had little concern for others and much self-centeredness. Through our economics project...[we] funneled their awareness of the vast differences in dwelling places of people and animals, and gave them a new sense of concern and caring for others (Kimbro, Freeman, and Tennison, 1994, p. 2).

Another example of a thematic unit, designed by a classroom teacher, is "Friends" (see Figure 4.11). This unit, designed by Terry Smith, a first–grade teacher from Harrisburg, Arkansas, emphasizes the areas of mathematics, science, and language arts.

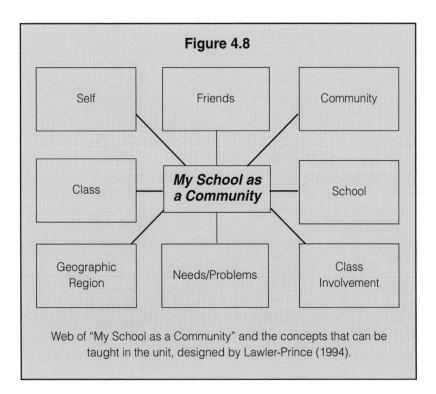

Figure 4.8

Self

Friends

Community

Class

My School as a Community

School

Geographic Region

Needs/Problems

Class Involvement

Web of "My School as a Community" and the concepts that can be taught in the unit, designed by Lawler-Prince (1994).

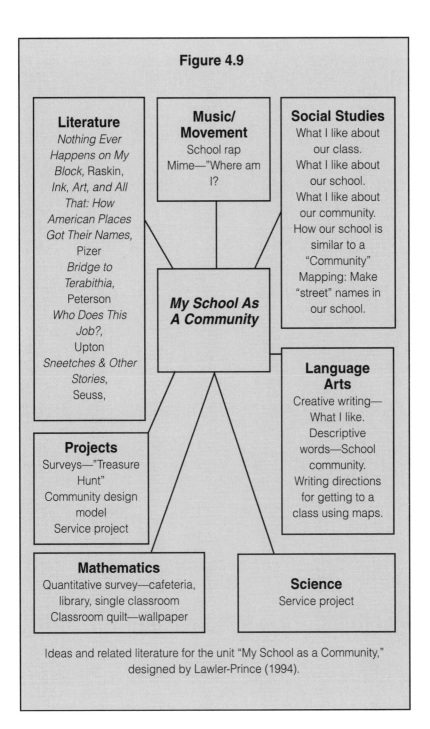

Figure 4.9

Literature
Nothing Ever Happens on My Block, Raskin, *Ink, Art, and All That: How American Places Got Their Names,* Pizer *Bridge to Terabithia,* Peterson *Who Does This Job?,* Upton *Sneetches & Other Stories,* Seuss,

Music/ Movement
School rap
Mime—"Where am I?

Social Studies
What I like about our class.
What I like about our school.
What I like about our community.
How our school is similar to a "Community"
Mapping: Make "street" names in our school.

My School As A Community

Language Arts
Creative writing— What I like.
Descriptive words—School community.
Writing directions for getting to a class using maps.

Projects
Surveys—"Treasure Hunt"
Community design model
Service project

Mathematics
Quantitative survey—cafeteria, library, single classroom
Classroom quilt—wallpaper

Science
Service project

Ideas and related literature for the unit "My School as a Community," designed by Lawler-Prince (1994).

Figure 4.10

Subtopics	Activities/Content Areas	Additional Ideas and Activities
Why study economics?	*Stuck in the Mud*, big book by J. Croser and J. Vassillou "If I only had a Brain," *Swimmy*, by Leo Lionni. To teach "cooperation." Homes for people—capital, human, and natural resources.	
Homes for animals— wants, scarcity, and decision making	*The Mitten*, a Ukrainian folktale. Categorizing animals. Decision-making—name the animals. A guest speaker from the Humane Society. *The Three Little Pigs*. Teaching concept of basic shelter.	
Home for people— capital, human, and natural resources.	"Priority Line" of wants. *The House that Jack Built*, a rebus book designed by Elizabeth Falconer. Categorizing resources by human resources, capital resources, and natural resources.	Field trip to observe different types of homes in our city
Where do we live? Postal worker, producer of services/ goods, and consumers	*The Post Office Book* by Gail Gibbons. Mail is delivered to our homes by postal workers. Assembly line to produce students' own stationery. Set up the classes as postal service.	
Homes in the past and around the world— wants and scarcities.	*In My Mother's House* by Ann Nolan Clark. Children learn through literature, guest speakers, and videos that people in other parts of the world have different wants.	

66

Figure 4.10—continued

Homelessness: scarcity and decision making	*Fly Away Home* by Eve Bunting. Children learn that changes and scarcities cause people and animals to make choices.	Community service—food drive. Field trip to the Mission Outreach Project. Decision making about selection of charity. Writing activity—"If I had $100, what would I do with it?"
Culminating activity—industrial park sleep-over: business factory, and money	*The Sneaker Factory* by JoAnne Nelson. Children learn about production through active participation in an assembly line. During the overnight school sleep-over, the children work in (classrooms remodeled into) "Happy Trash Recycling Center," "The Kookie Factory," "Tee-M Work Tee Shirt Factory," and "Wee Winter Workforce Factory."	Business person visits the classroom and brings an actual conveyor belt. Field trip to same business (Hytrol Conveyor Co.)
Spending the profits	*Berenstain Bears' Trouble with Money* by Stan Berenstain, and *Mud for Sale* by Brenda Nelson. Students exhibit a caring attitude as shown through journal writing, care of animals, recycling resources, and choosing to give profits from their company to help the homeless.	At the "Young Author's Fair," the children participating in this project designed house-shaped books. Community service—students raised over $500 from the sale of the product, refrigerator magnets. The money was given to the homeless project in their community.

Extensive thematic unit "There's No Place Like Home," designed by first- and second-grade teachers Karen Kimbro, Lois Freeman, and Candy Tennison (1994)

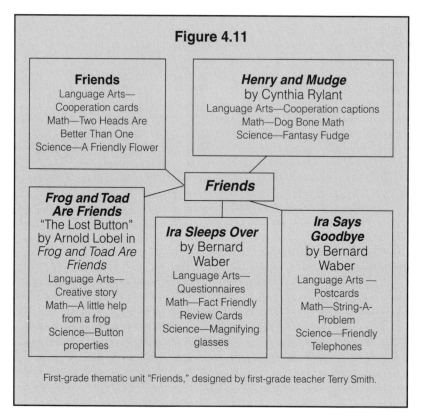

Figure 4.11

Friends
Language Arts—
Cooperation cards
Math—Two Heads Are
Better Than One
Science—A Friendly Flower

Henry and Mudge
by Cynthia Rylant
Language Arts—Cooperation captions
Math—Dog Bone Math
Science—Fantasy Fudge

Friends

Frog and Toad Are Friends
"The Lost Button"
by Arnold Lobel in
Frog and Toad Are Friends
Language Arts—
Creative story
Math—A little help
from a frog
Science—Button
properties

Ira Sleeps Over
by Bernard Waber
Language Arts—
Questionnaires
Math—Fact Friendly
Review Cards
Science—Magnifying
glasses

Ira Says Goodbye
by Bernard Waber
Language Arts —
Postcards
Math—String-A-
Problem
Science—Friendly
Telephones

First-grade thematic unit "Friends," designed by first-grade teacher Terry Smith.

Many other activities could be integrated into this unit as well. This is an example of one teacher's planning efforts, but it is a somewhat generic topic that could be used with different age groups and in various regions.

USING COMMUNITY RESOURCES

One of the key components in successful webbing and planning of thematic units is bringing together the needed resources. The term *resources* is used here to include the background knowledge of the students, people, and businesses in the community, potential field trips, and materials.

Business people realize that business has a tremendous stake in the education of young children, and they are usually eager to assist through guest speakers, tours of their factories or businesses, or sharing their products or materials with your classroom. Using this resource also enhances the communication between schools and businesses and can lead to more cooperation and understanding.

Many business organizations including the Chamber of Commerce and professional organizations like the National Association of Engineers or the Entomological Society of America have education committees or liaison officers whose job is to interface with local schools to enhance the program. These community resources are invaluable in planning thematic units.

Field trips can be successful forays into the community. They help students realize they are a part of a larger community (Ross and Roe, 1990). Many teachers think that successful field trips have to be far away from the location of the school. In reality, field trips can be to the supply room or the bus maintenance facility. Freiberg and Driscoll (1992) suggest that a field trip is only as successful as the teaching about the field trip that occurs prior to and following the trip itself.

Katz and Chard (1989) list several tips for effective field trips. The first is to make clear to the students the purpose of the field trip. Students have to know where they are going, how it ties in with what is taking place in the classroom, and what they are expected to observe and learn during the field trip. It is especially powerful to allow students to assist in planning the field trip. This helps the teacher build on students' background knowledge about the field trip topic and provides practical information about seats on a bus, permission slips, and so on. Ross and Roe (1990) find that field trips also help develop students' vocabulary.

Follow–up activities help students analyze what they observed and learned on the field trip. Suggested follow–up activities for field trips are writing, making Venn diagrams, discussing the trip, reading books, and making reports (Katz and Chard, 1989).

INCLUDING DEVELOPMENTALLY APPROPRIATE PRACTICES

In developing thematic units, teachers need to include practices that are developmentally appropriate for their students. Four practices that can be easily adapted to all ages of students are learning centers, cooperative learning structures, writing activities, and projects.

Pattillo and Vaughn (1992) define learning centers as "space where materials are organized in such a way that children

69

learn without the teacher's constant presence and direction" (p. 13). For kindergarten children, this usually means areas set aside for dress–up, blocks, kitchen plan, and so forth. In primary classrooms, learning centers often are related to an area of the curriculum, such as a folder game to reinforce letter recognition, a library corner with books to read, and a puppet center that has puppets related to a story read by students. Learning centers allow students to select many of their own activities and to work in small groups using concrete learning activities.

Kagan (1991), a developer and researcher of cooperative learning structures, describes the cooperative learning environment as one in which students work in small groups, but still have individual accountability, simultaneous interaction, and positive interdependence. During cooperative learning time, students work in small groups to complete tasks. Kagan has developed cooperative learning structures that can be used with students at any age and with any content area. Cooperative learning is powerful when used in conjunction with thematic teaching because it promotes leadership skills, working together toward common goals, and prosocial behavior—all important components of developmentally appropriate practices.

Writing activities can be powerful tools for engaging students. Tompkins (1994) says that writing, when used with thematic teaching, becomes a tool for learning. Writing "allows students to assume responsibility and ownership for their own learning" (p. 39). When students begin with a draft of their work, revise it, edit it, and publish it, they are able to see concrete results of their work. "Publishing children's written work in a final copy, printed edition, that is shared publicly is a powerful tool for motivating and engaging students in continued reading and writing" (Routman, 1991, p. 263).

A project may include creative dramatics, in–depth research, creative writing, and many other exploratory types of activities. A project could become a learning center in which children engage in these types of activities. One example of a project from Katz and Chard (1989) has young children design a "bus" after they have studied "Transportation." The teacher's role is to provide the necessary tools, space, and time. For example, the children might use a large cardboard box, yellow paint, and "pie pans" for headlights.

As emphasized in Chapter 1 of this book, developmentally appropriate practices promote learning that is meaningful and relevant to the lives of children. Thematic teaching is considered an integral part of developmentally appropriate practice.

REFERENCES

Baker, J. *The Impatient Gardener.* New York: Ballentine, 1983.

Berenstain, S. and Jan Berenstain. *Berenstain Bears' Trouble with Money.* New York: Random House, 1983.

The Biggest Pumpkin. New York: Holiday House Inc., 1984.

Bredekamp, S. (Ed.) *Developmentally Appropriate Practice in Early Childhood Programs Serving Children From Birth Through Age 8.* Washington, DC: The National Association for the Education of Young Children, 1992.

Brett, J. *The Mitten* New York: Morrow, William & Co., 1989.

Bunting, E. *Fly Away Home.* Boston: Houghton-Mifflin, 1991.

Campbell, M. "Powerful Learning Experiences." *The WEB: The Newsletter of Expeditionary Learning Outward Bound,* 2 (7), 2, 1994.

Clark, A.N. *In My Mother's House.* New York: Viking Children's Books, 1991.

Cousins, E. "Do Toads Go to Heaven?" *The Web: The Newsletter of Expeditionary Learning Outward Bound,* 1(2), 2., 1993.

———. (Ed.). "More Learning Expeditions in progress." *The WEB: The Newsletter of Expeditionary Learning Outward Bound,* 1(9), 6–7., 1993b.

Croser, J. and Vassillou, J. *Stuck in the Mud.* Dominguez Hill: Educational Insights, 1987.
Donnelly, L. *Dinosaur Garden.* (1991). New York: Scholastic Inc., 1990.

Ehlert, L. *Growing Vegetable Soup.* San Diego: Harcourt Brace &

Co., 1987.

Falconer, E.. *The House that Jack Built.* Nashville: Hambleton-Hill Publishing, 1990.

Freiberg, H.J., and Driscoll, A. *Universal Teaching Strategies.* Boston: Allyn and Bacon, 1992.

Gibbons, G. *The Post Office Book.* New York: Harper Collins Children's Books, 1982.

Henry and Mudge New York: MacMillan Children's Book Group, 1991.

Himmelman, J. *Amanda and the Magic Garden,* 1987.

Inkpen, M. *The Blue Balloon.* New York: Little, Brown & Co., 1990.

Kagan, S. *Cooperative Learning.* San Juan Capistrano, CA: Resources for Teachers, 1991.

Katz, L.G., and Chard, S.C. *Engaging Children's Minds: The Project Approach.* Norwood, NJ: Ablex, 1989.

Kimbro, K., Freeman, L., and Tennison, C. *There's No Place Like Home: A Whole Language Approach To Teaching Economics for the Primary Grades.* Grant project awarded by the Primary Division of the International Paper Company Foundation's National Awards for Teaching Economics, University Heights Elementary School, Nettleton Public Schools, Jonesboro, AR, 1994.

Kraus, R. *The Carrot Seed.* New York: Harper Collins Children's Books, 1989.

Krogh, S. *The Integrated Early Childhood Curriculum.* New York: McGraw-Hill, 1990.

Lawler-Prince, D. (1993, April). "Theory of Teacher Planning Styles." Presented as part of *Integrating the Curriculum: Child-Centered Activities for Primary Grade Teachers,* by D. Lawler-Prince, M.K. Cramer, J. Cramer, R. Towery, and M. McJunkin.

Paper presented at the annual conference of the Association for Childhood Education International, Phoenix, AZ, 1993.

Lawler-Prince, D., Cramer, M.K., Cramer, J., Towery, R., and McJunkin, M. *Integrating the Curriculum: Child-Centered Activities for Primary Grade Teachers.* Paper presented at the annual conference of the Association for Childhood Education International, Phoenix, AZ, 1993.

Lawler-Prince, D., Towery, R., Cramer, M.K., Cramer, J., and McJunkin, M. (1994, March). "Community Expeditions: A Journey into Learning." Paper presented at the annual conference of the Association for Childhood Education International, New Orleans, LA, 1994.

Lillegard, D. *Sitting in My Box.* New York: Puffin Books, 1993.

Lionni, Leo. "If I Only Had a Brain." In *Swimmy.* New York: Knopf Books for Young Readers, 1987.

Lobel, A. "The Lost Button." In *Frog and Toad Are Friends.* New York: Harper Audio, 1990.

Martin, B., Jr. *Brown Bear, Brown Bear, What Do You See?* New York: Holt, Henry, & Co., 1983.

McMillan, B. *Growing Colors.* New York: Lothrop, Lee and Shepard Books, 1988.

Nelson, B. *Mud for Sale.* Boston: Houghton-Miflin, 1984.

Nelson, J. *The Sneaker Factory.* Cleveland: Modern Curriculum Press, 1990.

Pattillo, J., and Vaughan, E. *Learning Centers for Child-Centered Classrooms.* Washington, DC: National Education Association, 1992.

Peterson, K. *Bridge to Terabithia.* New York: Crowell, 1977.

Pizer, V. *Ink, Art and All That: How American Places Got Their Names.* New York: Putnam, 1976.

Raskin, E. *Nothing Ever Happens on My Block*. New York: Scholastic, Inc., 1966.

Ross, E.P., and Roe, B.D. *An Introduction to Teaching the Language Arts*. Fort Worth: Holt, Rinehart, and Winston, 1990.

Routman, R. *Invitations: Changing as Teachers and Learners K–12*. Portsmouth, NH: Heinemann, 1991.

Rylant, Cynthia. *Henry and Mudge*. New York: Bradbury Press, 1987.

Seuss, T. *Sneetches and Other Stories*. New York: Random House, 1961.

Shores, E.F. *Exploring the Gulf Coast with Young Children*. Little Rock: Southern Early Childhood Association, 1993.

Three Little Pigs. New York: Arrow Trading Co.,1991.

Tompkins, G.E. *Teaching Writing: Balancing Process and Product*. New York: Merrill, 1994.

Upton, P. *Who Does This Job?* Honesdale, PA: Boyds Mills Press, 1991.

Waber, B. *Ira Says Goodbye*. Boston: Houghton Mifflin, 1988.

——. *Ira Sleeps Over*. Boston: Houghton Mifflin, 1975.

Chapter 5:

BOOK SELECTION AND USE: THE SEEDS AND BULBS

"If you start with seeds, you must be prepared to wait a bit longer for your harvest." (Baker, 1983, p. 176). When you select a new book (one you have not previously used), you must be prepared to read it, analyze its contents, and then prepare the theme or web around its theme or concept.

"Perennials are a great investment in a home garden because they come up year after year without the need for replanting every spring, as for annuals" (Baker, 1983, p. 154). Some books, with quality content, may be used year after year, without a search for newer versions.

Using quality literature as the basis for curriculum integration can make the difference between a mediocre lesson and one that students will remember forever. For this reason, the literature should be chosen carefully. There are tried and true principles and guidelines to follow when selecting literature. This chapter will illustrate the principles and criteria for selecting quality literature and will list some of the resources available to access that literature.

PRINCIPLES OF SELECTING LITERATURE

Literally thousands of books are available for students and teachers. Selecting the most appropriate and highest quality literature for your classroom is an important task (Huck, Hepler, & Hickman, 1993; Lukens, 1990; Norton, 1995), yet it can be difficult.

The source of literature that is most easily accessible is the basal reading series. Publishers generally select literature for their reading series that is geared to the interests and developmental levels of students. In recent years, they have printed the complete text of the literature selections rather than an adapted version. The selections include works from all genres of literature: fiction, biography, and nonfiction. For example, in its third-grade anthology, the Houghton Mifflin basal reading series (1993) includes: eight narrative texts, six expository pieces, and nine poems. Each anthology is also organized around themes. The four themes used in Houghton Mifflin's third-grade anthology are Family Album, It's Magic, A Visit to the Southwest, and Beware! Trouble Ahead. This use of themes has enabled teachers to use the basal reading series as the organizer for thematic units that extend beyond the basal and to expose students to a variety of quality literature.

Although there are specific guidelines for selecting quality literature for each genre of literature, the focus here will be on general guidelines that apply to all literature. For selecting additional materials, the guidelines endorsed by the American Library Association are helpful. These guidelines include selecting quality materials that :

- have appropriate content,
- meet the needs and interests of the students,
- meet the curriculum needs of the school, and
- maintain a balance in the school collection (Huck, Hepler, & Hickman, 1993).

Appropriate Content

The most important aspect of content is the developmental level and interests of students. According to Huck, Hepler, and Hickman (1993), there are two reasons for stressing appropriate content: (1) "Most children's books have to be read at an appropriate age and stage in the development of a child or they will never be read" (p. 38) and (2) the power of literature to enable a reader to experience lives vicariously is unequaled. They note, however, that the content must be judged in terms of the quality of the writing. "Almost any subject can be written about for children depending on the honesty and sensitivity of its treatment by the author" (p. 39). The quantity of children's literature available today virtually guarantees that quality books are available on any subject, topic, or theme.

Teachers must read widely to improve their ability to identify quality children's literature and to find literature that is appropriate to their students. Literature lends itself to teaching concepts and teachers must identify the concepts that are appropriate to the specific piece of literature. For example, as noted in Chapter 4, *Brown Bear, Brown Bear, What Do You See?* by Bill

Martin, Jr., (1983) is an appropriate book for teaching colors, but not for teaching about bears.

Needs and Interests of Students

When educators select materials, they must take into account the needs and interests of individual students in the broadest sense. Students with special needs as well as those with culturally diverse backgrounds must be represented in all phases of the curriculum. A "heightened sensitivity to needs of all people in American society" (Norton, 1995, p. 560) must be reflected in the literature collection of each school. Each student deserves to see himself or herself reflected in books, as well as to read about children who reflect other racial, ethnic, religious, and cultural backgrounds. While research indicates that children can become involved in the story regardless of the culture portrayed (Altieri, 1993; Altieri, 1995), studies have also shown that children prefer stories about their own culture (Altieri, 1995; Barchas, 1971; Nelson, 1987). The books available to students should "give them insights into their own lives, but they should also have books to take them out of those lives to help them see the world in its many dimensions" (Huck, Hepler, & Hickman, 1993, p. 40).

Students will choose books and literature that interest them. What interests students changes with their age and developmental level. Students in the same class or grade level read at many levels and express diverse interests (Norton, 1995). Teachers have difficulty addressing this wide range of reading interests and developmental levels when the basal reading series is the entire reading program in a school. Thematic planning can help teachers meet these needs.

Davis (1993) says that "If we can engage young learners in the wonder of stories, perhaps they will see themselves as storytellers and will, by extension and in appreciation of the narrative process...begin to engage in the stories of others—the wonder of books" (p. 9).

During the preoperational stage of development, preschool and primary children like books that anthropomorphize and have repeated patterns (Russell, 1994). Books that particularly appeal include standards like *Mike Mulligan and His Steam Shovel* by V.L. Burton (1939) and fairy tales with repeated patterns.

As children grow older, they become more aware of other people around them and enjoy reading about children who are facing problems similar to theirs (Russell, 1994). Beverly Cleary, Judy Blume, and Gertrude Warner are authors who appeal to these children.

Needs of the Curriculum

When selecting materials, educators should not underestimate the importance of supporting the curriculum. Specific areas of the curriculum may require additional materials. This is particularly true when teachers rely less on the published textbooks for all of their curriculum and more on thematic units of study. With the assistance of the school librarian or media center specialist, the full range of materials can be available to teachers. The availability of quality materials, books, and nonprint materials makes thematic curriculum more inviting and possible for teachers and students.

Teachers will find two types of books—content and concept—available to fit their thematic units. Two examples of content books are *In the Small, Small Pond* by Denise Fleming (1993) and *The Fascinating World of Ants* by Angelo Julivert (1991). These books are conducive to thematic teaching about mathematics, science, or social studies. Two examples of books that lend themselves to teaching about concepts are *Don't Forget to Write* by Martina Selway (1994) and *The Doorbell Rang* by Pat Hutchins (1994).

Balance in the School Collection

Those selecting children's literature are responsible for maintaining a balance in the collection by keeping in mind the needs of the total school (Huck, Hepler, & Hickman, 1993). This balance must be in terms of interest, all curricular areas, and developmental levels of students.

A balanced collection will include paperback books of high interest to students and nonprint materials that support the curriculum. Students may be interested in reading the "Goosebumps" series by R.L. Stine. They are a perfect choice for paperback collections, as are other books that become very popular among students for a short period of time and then are forgotten. Nonprint materials that support the curriculum may include videotapes, filmstrips, and student-produced media.

The library/media center collection in a school should contain some standards in children's literature. These include books by perennial favorites, such as Eve Bunting, Beverly

Cleary, Dr. Seuss, or Judith Viorst. The classics in children's literature should also be included. Among these are books by Beatrix Potter and E.B. White. (For a selection of titles by these authors, see **Additional Resources** on page 100.) A library/media collection should have periodicals as well as reference books.

A balance is necessary if teachers and students are to have access to quality children's books and other materials for developing their webs and pursuing their interests. Those making book selections must also consider the developmental level of students. Collections should have literature that is appropriate for all students. This requires careful choices on the part of the library/media specialist with input from students and teachers (Norton, 1995).

FINDING QUALITY LITERATURE

There are four major sources for finding quality literature: book review journals, lists of books published by professional organizations, lists of books that have earned awards, and bibliographies of children's literature. The most valuable sources for finding quality literature are the national and regional book review journals. Each of the journals takes a different perspective on the materials it reviews. One of the most comprehensive journals is the *School Library Journal*. All the reviews are written by professionals in the field of children's literature. The reviews tend to emphasize the literary elements (Norton, 1995) and the usefulness of a book to students and teachers (Cullinan, 1981). The *School Library Journal* reviews virtually all of the children's books published each year. Starred reviews mark those of the highest quality. (For a list of related journals, see **Additional Resources** on page 102.)

The *Booklist and Subscription Books Bulletin* publishes reviews only for those children's books that it recommends for purchase, approximately 45 per issue. It is published twice monthly and also includes reviews of books for adults.

Two other review journals are the *Horn Book* and the *Bulletin of the Center for Children's Books (BCCB)*. The *Horn Book* is published monthly and includes articles of interest to those involved in children's literature as well as book reviews. *BCCB* is published monthly and includes reviews of books and nonprint materials.

Regional book review publications review fewer books,

but they still provide a valuable service because they reflect the region in which they are published. One of these is *Sparks: A Review Journal of Children's Books for the Mid–South*. It is published quarterly by Arkansas State University and includes both positive and negative reviews of children's books. In addition to the book reviews, the journal includes a "Sparkler," which inspires teachers with ideas on thematic webbing.

Lists published by professional organizations are good sources of children's books. The International Reading Association (IRA) publishes a yearly list of books voted as best by a cross section of students. It is called "Children's Choice" and is published in the October issue of *The Reading Teacher*. In addition to the list published by the IRA, the National Science Teachers' Association and the National Council of Social Studies publish a yearly list of recommended children's books in each of their areas of specialty. There are many excellent sources that can help teachers locate literature about people of color (e.g., Bishop, 1992; Day, 1994; Lindgren, 1991). These sources can provide a wealth of information.

A third category of sources for quality books is the list of annual book award winners. The most prominent awards are the John Newbery Medal and Randolph Caldecott Award Medal. The Newbery Medal is awarded annually for the most distinguished contribution to literature for children in America. It was established in 1922 in honor of John Newbery, who was the first English publisher of books for children. The Caldecott Medal has been awarded annually since 1938 to the illustrator(s) of the most distinguished picture book for children in America. Randolph Caldecott was a nineteenth century illustrator of children's books.

The Coretta Scott King Award has been presented annually since 1970 to an African–American author and an African–American illustrator for outstanding inspirational and educational contributions to children's literature. Books whose authors or illustrators have received this award are generally appropriate for elementary and middle school students (Tompkins and McGee, 1993).

Children's literature bibliographies are a fourth source for finding quality literature. The bibliographies have a variety of purposes. The *Children's Catalog* helps teachers make a balanced selection of quality books for elementary schools. The various editions of *Book Finder* contain extensive lists of books appropriate for students who have special circumstances, for example, a death in the family, divorce, or other crisis. Another bibliographic source of books is *Interracial Books for Children* published by the Council on Interracial Books for Children. This is an annotated bibliography of recommended books on minorities in American culture with African Americans being the most heavily represented. Other sources of annotated lists of children's books are listed in Norton's (1995) *Through the Eyes of a Child: An Introduction to Children's Literature.*

USING MULTICULTURAL LITERATURE

According to Bishop (1992), multicultural literature is "by and about people who are members of groups considered to be outside the socio–political mainstream" (p. 39). Multicultural trade books generally include people of color from the United States, for example, African Americans, Native Americans, Hispanics, and people of color from other countries, for example, Asians, Africans, and Caribbeans. Multicultural trade books include all genres and books for all ages.

Teachers need to be aware of the categories of multicultural literature in order to integrate children's literature more effectively into the curriculum and experiences of students in their classes. Bishop (1992) organizes multicultural literature into three categories: generic, neutral, and specific.

Generic (or universal) multicultural trade books have main characters who are members of minority groups but have few or no specific "details that might serve to define those characters culturally" (p. 45). Trade books in the culturally *neutral* category "feature people of color, but are fundamentally about something else" (p. 46). A *specific book* "illuminates the experiences of growing up a member of a particular, non–white cultural group." (p. 44). Trade books that are specific may include details that are recognizable to members of the group. Details may be included in the "language styles and patterns, religious beliefs and practices, musical preferences, family configurations and relationships, social mores" (p. 44) among others. Specific books are the most powerful tools in assisting children in understanding people of color.

Teachers should also be aware of criteria to consider when evaluating multicultural literature. Various sources can provide specific ideas (Bishop, 1992; Latimer, 1972; Norton, 1991), but the teacher must select texts that are quality literature as well as an accurate representation of the culture portrayed.

USING LITERATURE IN WEBBING AND IN THEMATIC UNITS

Bone, Grymes, and Lawler–Prince (1992), developed a web based on multicultural literature, but they designed the web in a nontraditional way. The web was developed around the topic "People" and included the subtopics of "Me" (self–concept), "Family", "Community," and "World" (Figure 5.1).

The concepts addressed under Community were: (1) daily activities, (2) cooperation, (3) social justice, and (4) responsibilities. The concept of responsibility was further developed by the underlying themes of: (1) personal responsibility (how individuals can help the world); (2) family responsibility (family's responsibility to the environment); and (3) community responsibility (benefits other groups in the community) (Bone, Lawler-Prince, & Grymes, 1993a).

Community, a part of the broad unit "People," could be taught as a separate thematic unit or combined with the other themes as stated above. The web was designed to include subtopics, any of which could be further designed as a single thematic unit.

Bone, Lawler-Prince, and Grymes (1993b) recommend that Peter Spier's (1980) book *People* be used as a springboard. The book presents the premise that all persons, families, and communities have similarities and differences. Thus, the children will absorb principles of multiculturalism in an authentic context, learning about themselves, their families, and communities, rather than in contrived lessons about multiculturalism itself. (Bone et al, 1992, p. 34)

Other themes can be developed in which multicultural concepts are taught within the broad spectrum of the topic and concepts included in the unit. Multicultural concepts should be taught as a part of all curricular areas, rather than as a separate topic or issue (Derman–Sparks, 1989).

SUMMARY

Selecting literature appropriate to students' needs and interests and the content or concepts being taught is more difficult than it looks. Teachers need to read a wide variety of children's books and begin to share them with their students.

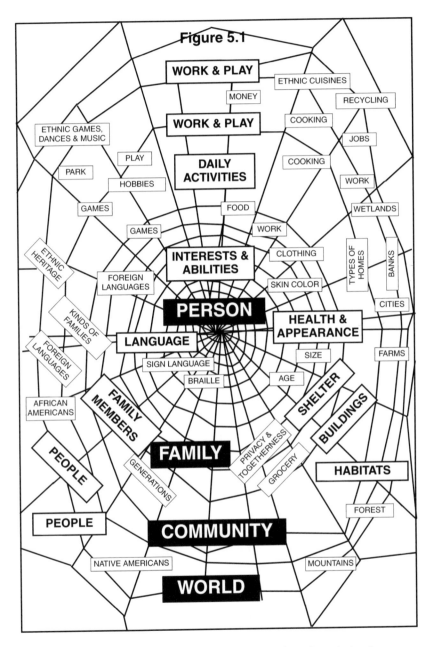

Figure 5.1

WORK & PLAY

ETHNIC CUISINES

MONEY

RECYCLING

WORK & PLAY

COOKING

ETHNIC GAMES, DANCES & MUSIC

JOBS

PLAY

DAILY ACTIVITIES

COOKING

PARK

HOBBIES

WORK

GAMES

FOOD

WETLANDS

GAMES

WORK

ETHNIC HERITAGE

INTERESTS & ABILITIES

CLOTHING

TYPES OF HOMES

BANKS

FOREIGN LANGUAGES

SKIN COLOR

KINDS OF FAMILIES

CITIES

PERSON

HEALTH & APPEARANCE

FOREIGN LANGUAGES

LANGUAGE

FARMS

SIGN LANGUAGE

SIZE

AFRICAN AMERICANS

BRAILLE

AGE

FAMILY MEMBERS

SHELTER

BUILDINGS

PEOPLE

FAMILY

PRIVACY & TOGETHERNESS

GENERATIONS

GROCERY

HABITATS

PEOPLE

FOREST

PEOPLE

COMMUNITY

NATIVE AMERICANS

MOUNTAINS

WORLD

Source: Bone, Grymes, Lawler-Prince, "Spinning culture through curriculum," Dimensions of Early Childhood (Fall 1992, p.33), Southern Early Childhood Association. Reprinted by permission.

Teachers' use of quality literature can improve thematic planning and increase student interest and literacy. Teachers should also maintain and periodically update a list of the books (resources) used when teaching each thematic unit. This organization of materials will help when planning future units.

REFERENCES

Altieri, J. L. "African–American Stories and Literary Responses: Does a Child's Ethnicity Affect the Focus of a Response?" *Reading Horizons.* 33, 236–244, 1993.

Altieri, J. L. "Multicultural Literature and Multiethnic Readers: Examining Aesthetic Involvement and Preferences for Text. *Reading Psychology: An International Quarterly,* 16, 43–70, 1995.

Baker, J. *The Impatient Gardener.* New York: Ballentine, 1983.

Barchas, F.E. "Expressed Reading Interests of Children of Different Ethnic Groups" (Doctoral dissertation, University of Arizona, 1971. *Dissertation Abstracts International,* 32, 2294A, 1971.

Bishop R. S. "Evaluating Books by and about African–Americans." In M. V., Lindgren (Ed.), *The multicolored mirror; Cultural Substance in Literature for Children and Young Adults,* 31–44, Fort Atkinson: Highsmith Press, 1991.

———— "Multicultural Literature for Children: Making Informed Decisions." In V. Harris (Ed.), *Teaching multicultural literature in grades K–8,* 38-53 Norwood: Christopher–Gordon, 1992.

Bone, S.F., Grymes, J.M., and Lawler–Prince, D. "Spinning Culture through Curriculum/a Multiculture Web: Part I." *Dimensions,* 21(1), 32–36, 1992.

Bone, S.F., Lawler–Prince, D. and Grymes, J.M., "Spinning Culture through Curriculum/a Multiculture Web: Part II" *Dimensions,* 21(2), 21–24, 1993.

———— "Spinning Culture through Curriculum/A Multiculture Web: Part III" *Dimensions,* 21(3), 26–32, 1993.

Burton, V.L. *Mike Mulligan and His Steam Shovel*. Boston: Houghton Mifflin, 1939.

Cullinan, B.E. *Literature and the Child*. San Diego: Harcourt Brace Jovanovich, 1981.

Davis, F.K. *A Narrative Approach to the Integration of Primary Level Curriculum*. Paper presented at the Annual Meeting of the Mid–South Educational Research Association, New Orleans, Louisiana, 1993.

Day, F. A. *Multicultural Voices in Contemporary Literature: A Resource for Teachers*. Portsmouth: Heinemann, 1994.

Derman–Sparks, L. *Anti–bias Curriculum: Tools for Empowering Young Children*. Washington, DC: National Association for the Education of Young Children, 1989.

Fleming, D. *In the Small, Small Pond*. New York: Holt, Henry & Co., 1993.

Houghton Mifflin Reading Series Boston: Houghton Mifflin, 1993.

Huck, C. S., S. Hepler, and J. Hickman *Children's Literature in the Elementary School* (5th ed.). Fort Worth: Harcourt Brace Jovanovich College Publishers, 1993

Hutchins, P. *The Doorbell Rang*. New York: William Morrow and Co., 1994.

Julivert, A. *The Fascinating World of Ants*. Hauppauge: Barons Educational Series, 1991.

Latimer, B. I. *Starting out Right: How to Choose Books about Black People for Young Children*. Madison: Madison Equal Opportunities Commission. ERIC Document Reproduction Service No. 065 656. 1972.

Lindgren, M. V. *The Multicolored Mirror; Cultural Substance in Literature for Children and Young Adults* (31–44). Fort Atkinson: Highsmith Press, 1991.

Lukens, R. J. *A Critical Handbook of Children's Literature.* Oxford: Harper Collins Publishers, 1990.

Martin, B.,Jr. *Brown Bear, Brown Bear, What Do You See?* New York: Holt, Henry & Co., 1983.

Nelson, G. L. "Culture's Role in Reading Comprehension: A Schema Theoretical Approach." *Journal of Reading,* 30, 424–429, 1987.

Norton, D. E. *Through the Eyes of a Child: An Introduction to Children's Literature.* (4th ed.) New York: Merrill Publishing Company, 1995.

Russell, D.L. *Literature for Children: A Short Introduction.* 2nd ed. New York: Longman, 1994.

Selway, M. *Don't Forget to Write.* Nashville: Hambleton-Hill, 1994.

Spier, P. *People.* New York: Doubleday & Co., 1980.

Stine, R.L. *Goosebumps: The Haunted Mask.* New York: Scholastic, Inc., 1993.

Tompkins, G. E. and L. M. McGee *Teaching Reading with Literature: Case Studies with Action Plans.* New York: Merrill, 1993.

Chapter 6

HARVESTING YOUR IDEAS FROM THE GARDEN

Some people harvest their squash and make a casserole, others freeze it, and still others make zucchini bread. Individuals make decisions based on guidance from all sources available to them. Just as gardeners make choices with their harvest, teachers make choices with their classrooms and they base their decisions on the information available to them.

Baker (1983) in *The Impatient Gardener* says "When winter comes, don't just walk away from your garden. Say farewell to the last of your vegetable friends and clean up your garden patch. Pull up any remaining plants and put them in your compost pile. If you are going to use the same plot next year, you can get a head start by applying lime, gypsum, and fertilizer now, before the snow comes. Then turn the soil and let it brew over the winter, and start over again next spring" (p. 180).

Your thematic plans *can* be used again next year, but you should spend some time reflecting, making notes, and identifying strengths and weaknesses based on this year's implementation. Next year, you can re-examine these ideas and expand them, based on the children's background experiences, their interests, and their input. You may decide that "compost" based on ideas from this thematic unit could be a starting point for a new or different unit next year. One of the many joys of teaching is its evolving nature.

SETTING REALISTIC GOALS

Derman-Sparks (1989) recommends "hastening with caution." Lawler-Prince recommends that preservice (beginning) teachers set goals, possibly aspiring to plan and teach two thematic units per semester during their first year of teaching. During that first semester, time may permit the planning of a third thematic unit that could be implemented during the spring of that first year of teaching. During the summer following the first year, teachers may re-examine the three planned units, break them into more units, or create additional units for their repertoires.

Another suggestion is finding at least one partner with whom to share ideas and brainstorm. Teachers in grade-level teams can do their planning together. As the team moves in similar directions, their efforts will be reduced.

The authors suggest that inservice teachers "hasten slowly" and set realistic goals. If a teacher is also a graduate student, has a family at home, and is involved in many community activities, the task of planning thematic units (at first) may seem to be insurmountable. If teachers choose a friend or colleague with whom to plan, the task can be cut in two. Attempting only one thematic unit per semester may be a good way to start—to build a foundation for further unit planning. Teachers who have been teaching for many years may have developed a tremendous repertoire of thematic units. Experienced teachers may also need to revitalize their units, or re-examine them. They may find gaps in concepts taught or subjects included, which will require further planning and implementing new activities and ideas.

KEEPING DEVELOPMENTALLY APPROPRIATE PRACTICES IN MIND

The crux of this book is developmentally appropriate practices. The suggestions made are in keeping with practices recommended by the National Association for the Education of Young Children (Bredekamp, 1987). All teachers want what is best and appropriate for their students. When they examine these practices, plan and implement them, and evaluate their outcomes, the result is effective teaching and learning.

Personalizing the thematic unit is also important. For example, anyone could implement the thematic unit described in Chapter 4 of this book, "My School as a Community." The personalizing (or creative adaptation) of this unit makes it more enjoyable to teach, as well as interesting and fun for the participants. Personalizing teaching is one facet of the teaching profession that makes it unique and stimulating.

When a group of teachers is committed to thematic teaching and motivated to plan and teach the topic, group members can create extensive thematic units, such as the award-winning unit that Kimbro, Freeman, and Tennison (1994) developed. "There's No Place Like Home," discussed in Chapter 4, won them a professional award, but the authors felt that the personal reward—seeing the children learn about giving and community service—outweighed the professional recognition they received.

BEGINNING TO USE THEMATIC TEACHING

Many teachers think that thematic planning and teaching is too difficult. Therefore, they do not attempt it. It can seem overwhelming at first, but you must start somewhere.

When Cousins (1993) asked Ron Berger, a sixth-grade teacher from Shutesbury, Massachusetts, "How do you start designing a thematic unit?" Berger said that he begins by selecting the topic, and within that theme or topic, he determines a number of projects that can occur under the study of this specific topic. Berger, who is a member of the Expeditionary Learning Outward Bound Teacher Advisory Board, also said that the selected theme must be designed to "suit the class," it must address the local culture, and should also suit the teacher's own interests and strengths.

As recommended in Chapter 4, you should reflect on your current planning style and on whether or not this is the planning style you would like to pursue. Then go with the style, or try a new one. Sometimes change can be a very refreshing and motivating experience! Once you set about your plan, stop periodically to reflect upon your direction, asking yourself whether or not you are pleased with what you have accomplished and what additional goals you want to set for yourself.

Once the plans are in place, if you are not working with a partner, ask a friend or colleague to examine and discuss the plans that you have made. A second opinion can always add a fresh perspective.

Berger (Cousins, 1993) further recommends examining the school day and the elements of the day that are contained within the theme. Learning as much as possible about the topic or concept should be the next step. Gathering resources and making written plans comes next. Looking for possible experts, guest speakers, and field trips should also be a part of this phase of planning. Thinking about possible projects is another important aspect of planning the thematic unit. Although the teacher designs the projects, the children who are working on them should maintain "ownership" (Katz & Chard, 1989).

Berger (Cousins, 1993) recommends that teachers begin planning for assessment by thinking of it in terms of self-assessment (by the children). Additional methods of assessment that could be incorporated are peer conferences, group critiques, self-editing and numerous drafts, written reflection sheets, and final presentations or performances. Kamii (1994) says that "once the unity between assessment and instruction is grasped, teachers no longer have to view one as taking time away from the other" (p.1). In the Expeditionary Learning project, teachers assume a tremendous amount of the critical responsibilities for designing teaching, promoting "love for learning," and developing appropriate assessment. "An important part of instruction will be to have students articulate, think about, and weigh standards through discussions among themselves" (p. 6).

In other words, to have a high level of implementation (of thematic teaching) traditional practices must be re-examined and, most probably, changed to more innovative, appropriate ones. Also, teachers must take responsibility for the types of assessments they use and stand behind those decisions.

Kamii and Keem (1993) state that "assessments should be opportunities to think and to learn as well as to demonstrate acquisition of significant knowledge and skills" (p. 7). Routman (1991) says it best:

> Teachers and administrators are constrained by course objectives and state guidelines. Some of these are necessary to ensure that important concepts are developed in logical sequence at particular grade levels. However, many districts further constrain educators by adopting basal texts and social studies and science textbooks using publishers' guidelines as a total program. These texts should be used as one of many resources to be referred to, not adhered to. (p. 293)

OVERCOMING OBSTACLES

All schools and classrooms have obstacles that must be overcome. The curriculum mandated by a state, the goals and objectives selected by a school district, and a teacher's style and preference can all affect the success of a thematic unit.

Again, teachers who give up before trying miss the rewards of thematic teaching. Seeing children's faces light up, as they do when learning is joyful and exciting, may be one of the greatest advantages of thematic teaching. Planning as a team, exploring possibilities, and using creative energies are just a few of the enjoyable benefits of thematic planning and teaching.

Teachers who are committed to the notion of thematic teaching can begin by going to the school district administrators and opening a dialogue about it. School districts may want to consider changing to thematic teaching gradually, one grade level at a time. Many kindergarten teachers have employed this method for years; they might begin working with primary grade teachers and assisting them in developing appropriate themes, activities, projects, and even selecting literature to accompany the thematic study.

School districts may also want to examine the many types of grant funding available for assisting in the process of change. The Expeditionary Learning project is funded by Outward Bound, an organization that strives to help people realize their potential through outdoor adventures. A portion of the funds are used for "mini-sabbaticals" during which teachers plan their "expeditions" (extensive thematic units) and then present them to their peers, the school administrators, and parents and community members. Although school districts may not begin in such an ambitious manner, they might begin with the allocation of funds for release time for the planning of these valuable thematic units. Campbell (1994) also advocates that "school visits by teachers afford the host school a particularly interested audience for student work, which in turn promotes self-reflection by host faculty and students" (p. 3). She further states that "if we really believe that experience is a powerful teacher, then orchestrating opportunities for teachers to share and learn from one another's successes and failures makes good sense" (p. 3).

ELIMINATING "I CAN'T"

Teachers must believe that they can plan and teach thematically. Teachers must begin to recognize their own strengths and abilities as professionals. Although the obstacles to thematic planning and teaching may be many, those who have tried and succeeded are always ready to discuss (and brag about) their successful experiences. An entire school district does not have to embrace the idea of thematic teaching for a single teacher, a group of teachers, or even an individual school to begin this process of teaching.

Creativity, as well as empowerment, is important for teachers if they are to maintain a positive outlook on their work. Teachers are decision makers, but when they lose touch with this important role, they may become passive, begin to feel lethargic, become unmotivated, and begin to feel powerless in the classroom. These teacher need to become rejuvenated, maybe through a support group (Routman, 1991), or by taking a class, or through professional reading. Once rejuvenated, a teacher may begin to try methods that he or she has not felt ready to try in the past.

The rewards of thematic teaching far outweigh the problems one may encounter when attempting this type of teaching. Thematic teaching may be the most creative, individualized method of teaching that you will try. Planning for thematic teaching may also cause you to do some of your highest-level thinking, so that you can teach it effectively. Even though Routman (1991) says she has never seen a truly integrated curriculum, it is certainly a worthy goal for you to be moving toward!

REFERENCES

Baker, J. *The Impatient Gardener.* New York: Ballentine, 1983.

Bredekamp, S. *Developmentally Appropriate Practice in Early Childhood Programs Serving Children From Birth Through Age 8.* Washington, DC: National Association for the Education of Young Children, 1987.

Campbell, M. "School Visits: An Expeditionary Approach to Professional Development." *The WEB: The Newsletter of Expeditionary Learning Outward Bound,* 2(3), 3, 1994.

Crail, K., Freeman, L., and Tennison, C. *There's No Place Like Home: A Whole Language Approach to Teaching Economics for the Primary Grades.* Grant Project awarded by the Primary Division of the International Paper Company Foundation's National Awards for Teaching Economics, University Heights

Elementary School, Nettleton Public Schools, Jonesboro, AR, 1994.

Cousins, E. "Expeditionary Learning in the Classroom: One Teacher's View. An Interview with Ron Berger." *The WEB: The Newsletter of Expeditionary Learning Outward Bound,* 1(1), 4–11, 1993.

Derman-Sparks, L. *Anti-bias curriculum: Tools for Empowering Young Children.* Washington, DC: National Association for the Education of Young Children, 1989.

Kamii, M. "Opportunity Favors the Prepared Mind: Integrating Assessment and Curriculum." *The Web: The Newsletter of Expeditionary Learning Outward Bound,* 2(1), 1, 6-7, 1994.

Kamii, M., and Keem, M. "Beginning the Conversation: Assessments in Expeditions." *The Web: The Newsletter of Expeditionary Learning Outward Bound,* 1(8), 7-9, 1993.

Katz, L.G., and Chard, S.C. *Engaging Children's Minds: The Project Approach.* Norwood: Ablex, 1989.

Routman, R. *Invitations: Changing as Teachers and Learners K-12.* Portsmouth: Heinemann, 1991.

BIBLIOGRAPHY

Bromley, K.D. *Webbing with Literature: Creating Story Maps with Children's Books.* New York: Harper Collins College Publishers, (1991). Designed to give ideas to K-8 teachers who wish to use webbing in their classroom. Includes over 100 (many teacher-created) webs corresponding to specific children's books. Discusses a variety of literature, including books dealing with other cultures and people with disabilities. Suggests appropriate grade levels for the recommended books.

Cowles, M., and Aldridge, J. *Activity-Oriented Classrooms.* Washington, D.C.: National Education Association, (1992). Includes suggestions for enlisting the help of administrators and parents in setting up an activity-oriented classroom. Describes individually oriented and group oriented classroom activities and discusses activity-focused learning tied into the content areas. Includes a list of predictable books

Davidman, L. and Davidman, P.T. *Teaching with a Multicultural Perspective: A Practical Guide.* New York: Longman, (1994). Offers ideas for creating equity in schools with practical ideas for activities and lessons on topics ranging from teaching about Thanksgiving to interviewing ancestors. Explains how to create a multicultural curriculum that integrates social studies and science, and provides multicultural units that link environmental, global, and citizenship issues.

Derman-Sparks, L. *Anti-Bias Curriculum: Tools for Empowering Young Children.* Washington, DC: National Association for the Education of Young Children, (1989). Explains how to teach children to resist stereotyping and how to work with parents on these issues. Focuses on differences and similarities of culture and addresses gender identity and disabilities. Includes a worksheet, detailing stereotypes associated with gender, culture, and people of differing abilities. A checklist helps teachers analyze children's books for sexism and racism.

Dimidjian, V.J. *Play's Place in Public Education for Young Children.* Washington, DC. National Education Association, (1992). Focuses on the theory of play and its important implications for today's classrooms. Addresses the relevance of play and what types are appropriate for each age group in early childhood. Provides specific suggestions for the types of play to implement in elementary classrooms and the teacher's role in doing so. An excellent resource for kindergarten as well as primary grade teachers.

Fredericks, A.D., Meinbach, A.M., and Rothlein, L. *Thematic Units: An Integrated Approach to Teaching Science and Social Studies.* New York: Harper Collins College Publishers, (1993). Explains how thematic units are designed and the relationship between the thematic approach and whole language. Presents science and social studies thematic units appropriate for primary level and intermediate level students.

Grace, C. and Shores, E.F. *The Portfolio and its Use: Developmentally Appropriate Assessment of Young Children.* Little Rock: Southern Association on Children Under Six, (1992). Shares ideas for developing an assessment portfolio for young children. Details how to use the portfolio in evaluation and how parents of young children can use portfolios. Provides a summary of assessment instruments and other resources that may be used in order to learn more about appropriately assessing young children. Appendixes include a checklist, activity chart, anecdotal record form, and a systematic record form.

Kamii, C., Manning, M., and Manning, G. (Eds.). *Early Literacy: A Constructivist Foundation for Whole Language.* Washington, D.C.: National Education Association, (1991). Presents the theory of constructivism in a very readable manner. Provides a study comparing Spanish-speaking and English-speaking children's spelling. Compares the New Zealand method of teaching reading to the way it is taught in the United States. Suggests a variety of developmentally appropriate assessment procedures that might be used in assessing early literacy.

Katz, L.G., and Chard, S.C. *Engaging Children's Minds: The Project Approach.* Norwood, New Jersey: Ablex Publishing Corporation, (1989). Emphasizes the value of teaching young children through projects for teachers with varying degrees of experience. Provides necessary background for those unfamiliar with the project approach. Offers specific suggestions those experienced with the project approach can use in their classrooms.

Details the research behind the philosophy.

Kostelnik, M.J., Howe, D., Payne, K., Rohde, B., Spalding, G., Stein, L., and Whitbeck, D. (Eds.), *Teaching Young Children Using Themes*. Santa Monica: Good Year Books, (1991). Designed for teachers of two-to-six-year-olds. Features four parts: social studies, science, language arts, and mathematical concepts. Chapters deal with different themes and detail facts teachers may wish to teach along with practical classroom activities. Provides a list of children's books pertaining to each theme.

Krogh, S. *The Integrated Early Childhood Curriculum*. New York: McGraw-Hill Publishing Company, (1990). Details the reasoning behind curriculum webs and how to begin them. Deals with different content areas, explaining why they should be integrated and what the teacher's role should be within them. Provides ideas for explaining the program to parents.

Manning, M.M., Manning, G.L., Long, R., and Wolfson, B.J. *Reading and Writing in the Primary Grades: A Whole-Language View*. Washington, D.C.: National Education Association, (1987). Describes how to construct a primary literacy program around a whole-language philosophy. Discusses numerous practices used to develop literacy and suggests ideas such as cooking, singing, and recorded read-alongs to enhance learning. Features one section devoted to young children's writing. Concludes with a list of predictable books, poetry collections, the authors' favorite books, and books that can be used with cooking activities.

Pattillo, J., and Vaughan, E. *Learning Centers for Child-Centered Classrooms*. Washington, D.C.: National Education Association, (1992). Designed to enable teachers to develop learning centers in their classrooms. Discusses everything from the physical arrangement of the classroom to the scheduling of the day. Explores issues such as monitoring center choices and settling conflicts with children. Shares in detail a number of preprimary and primary learning centers. Figures complement the text and make the learning center ideas easy to understand.

Roberts, P.L. A Green Dinosaur Day: *A Guide for Developing Thematic Units in Literature-Based Instruction*, K-6. Needham Heights, Massachusetts: Allyn and Bacon, (1993). Focuses on how to plan a thematic unit and incorporate literature into a variety of content areas. Provides ideas for classroom organizational plans, a section on meeting the needs of diverse students, and a chapter on assessing and evaluating students and oneself. Includes a chapter on research supporting literature-based instruction and provides activities and reproducibles.

Ross, E.P. *Using Children's Literature Across the Curriculum.* Bloomington, Indiana: Phi Delta Kappan Fastback, (1994). Includes guidelines for thematic studies as well as suggestions for literature in the content areas. Features a section on multicultural literature and its selection in thematic teaching. Provides lists of references along with resources. Helpful to primary grade teachers in the planning process.

Shackelford, K. and Wilson, M.*A Thematic Literature-Based Unit: Glad To Be Me and a Thematic Literature-Based Unit: Tails of the Sea.* Dallas, Texas: Lasting Lessons, (1992). Each of these two books discusses lessons that are developed around a piece of literature. Both attempt to integrate a variety of subject areas into specific lessons. Appendixes include necessary patterns and pictures for lessons. Units are designed to be used with pre-kindergarten through second grade students and to last approximately two weeks.

Shaw, J.M. *Growing and Learning: Ideas for Teachers of Young Children.* Little Rock Southern Association on Children Under Six, (1990). Provides information on the relevance of teaching with thematic units and the steps necessary to develop them. Suggests ideas for quality thematic unit activities that can be developed around themes such as dinosaurs, ourselves, or springtime. Details important considerations that teachers should keep in mind when working with young children.

Shores, E.F. Explorers' Classrooms: *Good Practice for Kindergarten and the Primary Grades.* Little Rock: Southern Association on Children Under Six, (1992). Stresses the importance of teachers making learning meaningful for children through relevant, child-centered classrooms. Portrays children as explorers who can make choices and decisions in what they want to learn. Text and photographs look at various schools located throughout the South.

Shores, E. F. *Exploring the Gulf Coast with Young Children: Authentic Activities and Projects for K-3 Classrooms.* Little Rock: Southern Early Childhood Association, (1993). Includes regionally appropriate activities for children who are familiar with the Gulf Coast region. Covers everything from fire ants to mollusks. Discusses a variety of reading material that can be used in the lessons, such as picture books, poetry, and Gulf Coast newspapers. Suggested activities include writing, map making, and field trips.

Thompson, G. *Teaching Through Themes.* New York: Scholastic Inc., (1991). Discusses themes such as people, friendship, habitats, courage, mystery, and survival along with specific books correlating with each theme. Provides a short synopsis for each text and details how the book can be tied into the theme. Features themes for younger and older children.

York, S. *Roots & Wings: Affirming Culture in Early Childhood Programs.* St. Paul, MN: Redleaf Press, (1991). Provides activities designed to teach about diverse cultures and clearly states the themes, goals, and materials that can be used to do so. Includes thought-provoking questions for each chapter. Includes a chapter on holidays and celebrations with discussion on how holidays can teach negative values and positive values. Explains how prejudice is formed and its effects.

ADDITIONAL RESOURCES

Books

Bunting, Eve. *A Day's Work*. Boston: Houghton Mifflin, (1994).

—. *Fly Away Home*. Boston: Houghton Mifflin., (1991).

—. *Happy Birthday, Dear Duck*. Boston: Houghton Mifflin, (1988).

—. *How Many Days to America?* A Thanksgiving Story. Boston: Houghton Mifflin, (1988).

—. *Just Like Everyone Else*. Boston: Houghton Mifflin, (1992)

Cleary, Beverly. *Beezus and Ramona*. New York: Morrow Junior Books, (1990).

—. *Dear Mr. Henshaw*. New York: Morrow Junior Books, (1992).

—. *Henry Huggins*. New York: Morrow Junior Books, (1950).

—. *Ralph S. Mouse*. New York: Morrow Junior Books, (1983).

—. *Ramona the Brave*. New York: Morrow Junior Books, (1984).

Potter, Beatrix. *Jemima Puddle-Duck*. New York: Warne, Frederick & Co., (1994).

—. *The Tailor of Gloucester*. New York: Warne, Frederick & Co., (1987).

—. *The Tale of Benjamin Bunny*. New York: Warne, Frederick & Co., (1987).

—. *The Tale of Mrs. Tittlemouse & Other Mouse Stories*. New York: Warne, Frederick & Co., (1985).

—. *The Tale of Peter Rabbit*. New York: Warne, Frederick & Co., (1987).

Seuss, Dr. (Theodor Seuss Giesel). *Bartholomew and the Oobleck.* New York: Random House Books for Young Readers, (1949).

——. *Fox in Socks.* New York: Random House Books for Young Readers, (1965).

——. *Green Eggs and Ham.* New York: Random House Books for Young Readers, (1960).

——. *There's a Wocket in My Pocket!* New York: Random House Books for Young Readers, (1974).

Viorst, Judith. *Alexander & the Terrible, Horrible, No Good, Very Bad Day.* New York: Macmillan Children's Book Group, (1972).

——. *Alexander, Who Used to Be Rich Last Sunday.* New York: Macmillan Children's Book Group, (1978).

——. *I'll Fix Anthony.* New York: Macmillan Children's Book Group, (1969).

——. *My Mama Says There Aren't Any Zombies, Ghosts, Vampires, Creatures, Demons, Monsters, Fiends, Goblins, or Things.* New York: Macmillan Children's Book Group, (1973).

——. *Rosie and Michael.* New York: Macmillan Children's Book Group, (1974).

Warner, Gertrude C. *The Boxcar Children.* Morton Grove, IL: Whitman, Albert & Co, (1992).

——. *Houseboat Mystery.* Morton Grove, IL: Whitman, Albert & Co., (1966)

——. *Mystery Behind the Wall.* Morton Grove, IL: Whitman, Albert & Co., (1973)

——. *Schoolhouse Mystery.* Morton Grove, IL: Whitman, Albert & Co., (1965).

White, E.B. *Charlotte's Web.* New York: Harper Collins Children's Books, (1952).

—. *Stuart Little*. New York: Harper Collins Children's Books, (1945).

—. *Trumpet of the Swan*. New York: Harper Collins Children's Books, (1970).

Journals

The Booklist. Published by the American Library Association, 50 East Huron, Chicago, IL 60611.

Bulletin for the Center of Children's Books. Published by Graduate Library School, University of Chicago Press, 5801 Ellis Ave., Chicago, IL 60637.

Horn Book. Published by Horn Book, Inc., Park Square Building, 31 James Ave., Boston, MA 02116.

The Reading Teacher. Published by the International Reading Association, 800 Barksdale Road, Newark, DE 19714.

School Library Journal. Published by R.R. Bowker and Co., P.O. Box 13706, Philadelphia, PA 19101.

Sparks. Published by Arkansas State University, Department of Elementary Education, P.O. Box 2350, State University, AR 72467.

Science and Children. Published by the National Science Teachers Association, 1840 Wilson Blvd. Arlington, VA 22201.

SPECIAL THANKS TO CONTRIBUTORS

The authors would like to express special thanks to those classroom teachers who contributed authentic examples for this publication.

Iyla Ant, Brenda Janco, Mary Kane, Christine McCarron, and Eleanor Ray of Table Mound Elementary, Dubuque Communicity School District, Expeditionary Learning Outward Bound Project, Dubuque, Iowa.

Jami Bridger, Pat Edgin, Janet Hagood, Marlene Shannon, and Sheila Taylor, former graduate students at Arkansas State University and currently classroom teachers.

Mona Broadway, a third-grade teacher at South Elementary School, Jonesboro Public Schools, Jonesboro, Arkansas.

Karen Kimbro, Lois Freeman, and Candy Tennison, first- and second-grade teachers at University Heights Elementary School, Nettleton Public Schools, Jonesboro, Arkansas.

Lisa Metz, first-grade teacher at Hillcrest Elementary, Jonesboro Public Schools, Jonesboro, Arkansas.

Kittie Mickle, a preservice teacher at Arkansas State University.

Jane Mills, Joyce Neff, Cheryl Reeves, Kimberly Rouse, and Kay Sloan, second-grade teachers at North Elementary School, Jonesboro Public Schools, Jonesboro, Arkansas.

Terry Smith, a first-grade teacher at Harrisburg Public Schools, Harrisburg, Arkansas.

Christi Zielinski, a preservice teacher at Arkansas State University.